ICE TO THE ESKIMOS

ICE TO THE ESKIMOS

How to Market a Product Nobody Wants

JON SPOELSTRA

HarperBusiness
A Division of HarperCollinsPublishers

HarperCollins books may be purchased for educational, business, or sales promotional use. For information please write: Special Markets Department, HarperCollins Publishers, Inc., 10 East 53rd Street, New York, NY 10022.

FIRST EDITION

Designed by Elina D. Nudelman

Library of Congress Cataloging-in-Publication Data

Spoelstra, Jon.
    Ice to the Eskimos : how to market a product nobody wants / by Jon Spoelstra. — 1st ed.
        p.   cm.
    "The NBA's top marketer shares his in-the-trenches secrets to jump-start your sales, excite your customers, and improve your bottom line."
    Includes index.
    ISBN 0-88730-851-1
    1. Marketing.   I. Title.
HF5415.S725   1997
658.8—dc21   97-1944

---

97 98 99 00 01 ❖/RRD 10 9 8 7 6 5 4 3 2 1

CONTENTS

ACKNOWLEDGMENTS

"One can't believe impossible things."

"I daresay you haven't had much practice," said the Queen. "When I was your age, I always did it for half-an-hour a day. Why, sometimes I've believed as many as six impossible things before breakfast."
> —Lewis Carroll, *Alice in Wonderland*

I thank all the people who allowed me to think impossible things. It all started, of course, with my mother and father. Then my wife, Lisa. My kids, Monica and Erik, made their contributions. Along the way was Larry Weinberg. He used to own the Portland Trail Blazers. He not only wanted me to think impossible things, he would take off his jacket and wave me on.

1. JUMP-STARTING OUT OF HELL

Ground rule #1: You've got to want to clip on the wires and turn up the juice.

I've spent almost twenty years as an executive for teams in the NBA. Of the four teams that I have worked for, I've seen over 250 players come and go. But the most charismatic player I've ever been associated with is a player you probably have never heard of: **Billy Ray Bates.**

Billy Ray joined the Portland Trail Blazers about halfway through the 1981–82 season. He was a 6'4", 200-pound shooting guard who had toiled in minor league basketball for a couple of seasons. Once he got the chance with us, he exhibited dunks that only a Dr. J or a Michael Jordan could even think about. And he shot the three-pointer like a Larry Bird. One season, he hoisted the Blazer team onto his shoulders and lugged them to a playoff birth. Then he averaged 27 points a game in the playoffs. The Portland crowd loved Billy Ray more than any other player I have ever seen, including Clyde Drexler.

Billy Ray's education was spotty at best. But he sure could

come up with some great one-liners. For instance, once when Billy Ray was being interviewed on our postgame radio show by Bill Schonely, the voice of the Blazers, Schonely asked him about his time in the CBA, basketball's minor league. Billy Ray said, "The CBA is a great street corner, but you can't hang around there for the rest of your life."

There are hundreds of other one-line responses by Billy Ray that we heard over the two and a half years he played for us. The best was when he was in the office one summer visiting Stu Inman, the Blazers director of player personnel. After the meeting, Billy Ray walked down the long hallway where our offices were. Stu called to him, "Billy, Billy Ray."

Billy Ray stopped right in front of my door. I looked up.

Stu yelled, "Did you see where Kentucky State [where Billy Ray starred in college] is dropping basketball?"

Without even a blink or a quick head fake, Billy Ray said, "Aw, shucks, now I won't have nothing to remember."

It sounded like Billy was referring to Communist Russia. You know, fall out of power and your name gets removed from the history books.

In reading this book, I think you'll have plenty to remember and implement. If you implement *just one* of the jump-start marketing principles, you'll be way ahead. If you implement a lot of the principles, you could even market ice to the Eskimos.

At the beginning of each chapter, I tell a little anecdote from my experiences in the NBA. Sometimes the anecdote is related to the chapter; sometimes it isn't. The anecdote is just an easy way to get into the chapter. If you need a small break from reading about the jump-start marketing principles in *Ice to the Eskimos*, skip ahead and read the anecdotes.

■

The principles of jump-start marketing began for me with a phone call at about 11:00 P.M. on a Sunday between Christmas and New Year's in 1991.

"This is Alan Aufzien," the caller said. "I'm the chairman of the New Jersey Nets."

Normally, you would answer, "Yes?" or something like that. Instead, I experienced one of those phenomenal thought processes where somehow we can think of a whole slew of things in just a *nanosecond.* In that nanosecond before I answered the chairman, I thought I was being set up by some students. You see, I had been teaching sports marketing at the University of Portland. To make a point on how *not* to do something, I always referred to the New Jersey Nets. For as long as I could remember, they had been the laughingstock of the NBA—both on and off the basketball court. To add some sick humor to the class, I would make some awful comment about their penchant for acquiring players who had problems with drugs. I would say, "The only thing that the Nets have led the league in were drug rehab cases." Sometimes I would add, "If the Nets couldn't draft another drug addict, they would trade for one. If that didn't work, they would sign one as a free agent."

When Alan identified himself, I immediately thought that some students had dreamed up a practical joke and got an adult to call and accuse me of always picking on the Nets. The tip-off was the time of day. At 11:00 P.M. in Portland, it was 2:00 A.M. in New Jersey. On a *Sunday* night. Little did I know at the time that the Nets would keep you up on any night of the week.

In that rush of thinking in that nanosecond, I had a perfect rejoinder to the students' practical joke on me. "What do you need, a new drug connection for your players?" As I started to say those words, I caught myself. I chickened out. I said, "Yes?"

As you would figure, it wasn't a practical joke. It was really the chairman of the Nets, and I didn't make a fool of myself.

"We would like for you to come and talk to us about some consulting," Alan said.

"I'm not interested," I said. After eleven years as senior VP/general manager with the Portland Trail Blazers (where I resigned) and then ninety days as president/GM of the Denver Nuggets (where I was fired), I was enjoying my career as an adjunct professor. You would, too. Think of the life I was leading.

Twice a week, I would go to the campus about noon. I would have lunch with some students. I would teach my class from 1:00 to 2:20. I would walk over to the student center and have a cup of coffee. After coffee, I would walk over to the basketball arena on campus and watch practice. After an hour or so, I would come home. My wife would ask, "Well, how was your day?" "Tough," I would say. "Really tough."

On days that I didn't teach, we would drive an hour and fifteen minutes to our beach house on the Oregon coast. *Really, really* tough.

"If you don't want to consult, could you at least come into New York for dinner with us and give us some advice?" Alan asked. "We'll pay all of your expenses, and a fee, of course. What would your fee be?"

I didn't want to go to New York to have dinner. The seven owners of the New Jersey Nets had a reputation for being cheap bastards, so I gave him an outrageous fee, plus first-class expenses to fly into New York to have dinner. I knew they wouldn't accept.

He said, "Okay, how about Wednesday night?"

The rest is history. Without that dinner, however, and the subsequent four and a half years marketing the Nets (2 years as a consultant, 2.5 years as president/chief operating officer),

I would never have really got to the true essence of jump-start marketing. I would have been just like any other marketing executive who did a decent job marketing a decent product. I had never before been so flat-out challenged as I was in marketing the Nets. I don't think any marketing executive in the history of the world has been so challenged. But without this huge challenge, I wouldn't have come to depend on the jump-start marketing techniques that I think are applicable to any product or any company in any field.

DO YOU NEED TO BE A FAN?

I use many examples from the world of marketing a sports team to illustrate my principles of jump-start marketing. Does this mean you have to be a sports fan to appreciate these marketing principles? Of course not. Don't mistake this book as a *sports marketing* book. After reading this book, you won't be able to run away and join a pro sports team. What you will be able to do is take the ideas and principles of jump-start marketing and quickly adapt them to your particular field.

If you are indeed a sports fan, I think you'll agree that the examples in this book are more fun to read—and the ideas can be more adaptable—than if I were writing about how to market steel or fertilizer, or sweat socks.

ARE THERE EASIER WAYS TO JUMP-START A COMPANY?

When you read the newspapers, it seems that others have found easier ways to jump-start a company. After all, almost daily you can read about a company laying off hundreds or even thousands of employees. In the short term, that probably works. The balance sheet will certainly look better. But this savings is just delaying what really needs to be done—*to jump-start the company through marketing.* With jump-start marketing, those employees might not need to be laid off in the first place.

Keeping employees also helps other companies. After all, employees are customers, too. When employees—*or customers*—get laid off, they usually "lay off" their spending. So when you read about a company laying off thousands of employees, you can say, "Thanks, pal, you just eliminated part of my market." It would be much better for us all if companies used jump-start marketing techniques to boost sales and profits.

So, with jump-start marketing you can help your company, your employees, other companies, our country, other countries, and the world. Now, why wouldn't you plug in and use some of these strategies and techniques and jump-start your company?

A Simple Test You Can Take

To assist you in adapting these principles to your company, I give you a little test at the end of each chapter. You don't send in your answers for a grade. Just take the test and let the ideas flow.

It's an open-book test, meaning that you can look back to the pages of each chapter for some of the answers. Some of the other answers aren't in the book; they are with you. These answers involve taking the principles of jump-start marketing and applying them to your particular business.

This first little test is the easiest. It has only one question to answer. And it's multiple choice, no less. However, if you don't pass this easy little test of one question, you should close the book, find the receipt, and see if you can return it to the bookstore where you bought it.

(Multiple choice.) I want to:

A. **Help jump-start the company I work for.**
B. **Help our employees perform better.**
C. **Help jump-start the national economy.**
D. **Help jump-start the world economy.**
E. **All of the above.**
F. **None of the above.**
G. **Use this information to help *downsize* my company.**

Answers

If you answered (E), you did terrific! Write 150 percent (that's on a scale of 100 percent). Take a look at that 150 percent; that's your grade! Better than the grade, you'll enjoy this book and be able to apply a lot of the principles of jump-start marketing. When you apply these principles, you'll see that they work, that your company experiences some important growth. You'll be a hero, and your employees will think of you as a saint.

If you answered (A) or (B), give yourself 120 percent. Not bad, eh? You see, if all you want to do is help jump-start the company you work for or help your employees perform better, you will accomplish both by using the principles of jump-start marketing. You'll also accomplish (C) and (D). You didn't get 150 percent because you didn't have the altruistic goals of (C) and (D).

If you answered (C) or (D), grade yourself 70 percent. You passed! However, be aware that you may be a little too altruistic. Altruism starts at home—in this case your company. If you jump-start your company and thousands upon thousands of others jump-start their companies, then (C) and (D) will naturally take care of themselves.

Flunking This Little Test?

If you answered (F), I don't quite understand your motivation for even reading this far, so your grade is *incomplete*. If you continue reading to the last page, then I recommend that you take this test again.

Lastly, if you answered (G), turn in your test and walk out the door. You must be a financial type that will be trying to learn the principles of jump-start marketing so that you can be a little knowledgeable when you try to kill company growth. Well, reading this book won't work for you. The book will just confirm your belief that all marketing people are crazy.

2. ULYSSES, YOU, AND ME

Ground rule #2: Don't fool yourself into thinking you're somebody else.

My son played professional basketball in Germany for a couple of years. Somewhere along the line, he and I sat down and he told me what he wanted to do for a living.

He took my course while I was an adjunct professor, so I knew he was bright and had a good work ethic. But, he told me, "Dad, I want to be a coach."

I sat and stared at him for a while.

"You know, Erik," I said, "if you came and told me that you had a drug habit, we would send you to rehab. If you told me that you were an alcoholic, we would get you dried out. But if you want to be a coach, there is nothing we can do for you."

Coaches are the craziest people I have ever met. When they win a game, they can't enjoy it, because they know they're going to lose the next one. When they lose a game, they think they might not ever win another one. In fact, one day Dream Team coach Chuck Daly came into my office when we were both with the Nets. The Nets had lost two straight games. Chuck said, "We might not win another game this season."

"Chuck, there's sixty games left! We're 8–14 right now. You think we're going to lose sixty straight and finish 8–74?"

"It could happen the way we're playing," Chuck said. "It could happen."

It didn't happen. We went on to win thirty-four games and lose twenty-six.

Regardless of what crazy future faces my son as a coach, at least he knows what he wants to do. He knows what he is, he knows where he is going. I find that the main problem for companies that have trouble marketing themselves is knowing who they are and what their market really is. If you think you know who you are and what your market really is, after reading this chapter you might see different pixels that change the whole image.

■

Most of us never get the chance to market the *best* product in the *best* market with the *biggest* advertising budget and the *biggest* market share. In fact, most of the time our products have warts and pimples in all the wrong places. Our job is, of course, to successfully market these products—warts, pimples, and all. I've had more than my share of these types of products, and the first thing I do in marketing such a product is to think of Ulysses.

ULYSSES, YOU AND ME

I can best explain how I use Ulysses by bringing you right into the middle of how we decided to market a woeful product—the New Jersey Nets. In fact, in this chapter I'm going to make you an *owner* of the Nets. As an owner of the Nets, you'll vividly see how I used Ulysses—and how you can use Ulysses—in marketing other less-than-the-best products.

As an owner of the New Jersey Nets, picture this. You're sitting at a table in a quiet, upscale Manhattan restaurant with two of your partners in the Nets. You sit facing me.

"Help us lure people from Manhattan to our games in New Jersey," one of your partners says to me over dinner.

"Forget Manhattan," I say. "Pretend like it's not even there."

You might be a little stunned. "Forget Manhattan?" you blurt out. "Our arena is only six miles from Manhattan through the Lincoln Tunnel! Most of the nation's biggest businesses are based in Manhattan. How can we just *forget* Manhattan?"

PRETEND YOU ARE ULYSSES

Okay, if you're really mesmerized by the power, strength, and numbers that are Manhattan, try this. *Don't* pretend that Manhattan isn't there. Instead, pretend to be Ulysses.

Remember, Ulysses was the guy who was captain of a ship thousands of years ago. He had heard stories about the Sirens. These Sirens sang such beautiful songs that boats would navigate closer and closer to hear. Then when they were totally entranced by the beautiful music, the boats would crash on the rocks and everyone would die.

Ulysses wanted to hear the Sirens' song, but he didn't want to crash on the rocks and die. So he took wax and plugged the ears of his sailors so they couldn't hear the song. Then he had himself strapped to the mast so that he could not get free. Thus he heard the song—it drove him momentarily crazy— but he didn't crash on the rocks and die.

So let's say that you heard the siren song of Manhattan. You saw the World Trade Center. You went to Trump Tower. You caught a play on Broadway. You experienced the thrill of a life-time barreling down Third Avenue in a cab. Sure, you were thrilled to hear the siren song of New York City, but more importantly, *your crew didn't.* You had put wax in their ears, and after hearing the siren song, you safely sailed on, the song becoming a distant memory.

In the case of the New Jersey Nets, you sailed on to where else but New Jersey. Seems logical, doesn't it? But let's take a look at the *reality* of the Nets product and its market: northern New Jersey. You'll see the importance of Ulysses.

Here's a quick scouting report on the product of the New Jersey Nets:

- **Dead last in sales.** Suppose you looked at a product that ranked twenty-seventh in sales from a universe of twenty-seven products? That's what you own. That's what I was looking at as a consultant to the Nets. For the five years before I had dinner with you and the other two Nets owners, the Nets were dead last in the NBA in gate receipts. They were so firmly last that there wasn't any team that was second to last. With that type of record, if finishing dead last was an honor, the Nets would have retired it and hung it up on the rafters of the arena.

- **Terrible product.** What if the toothpaste you were marketing tasted like gasoline? In the previous five years, the Nets either finished as the worst or second worst team in the NBA. Besides playing lousy basketball, the teams were filled with head cases with which no sane fan could identify. The record speaks for itself. Take a look.

Season	Won	Lost
1990–91	26	56
1989–90	17	65
1988–89	26	56
1987–88	19	63
1986–87	24	58

"Aha!" you might exclaim, "lousy team, lousy attendance. If you win, you will draw fans; if you don't win, you won't. I rest my case."

That *sounds* logical, but it is false. It has been proven many times that winning doesn't equate with sold-out arenas. Just like the best products don't automatically lead in sales and profits.

There are tons of examples, and not just in the United States. It's a world-wide phenomenon: If your team wins, you don't automatically sell out your arena or stadium. Ask the Atlanta Hawks. In the 1993–94 season, they had the best record in the Eastern Conference of the NBA. They were also second to last in paid attendance.

Ask the Seibu Lions, a baseball team in Japan. They won the Japanese championship seven out of eleven years. Their attendance, however, is mediocre.

Ask the Real Madrid pro basketball team. In the 1990s, they were the European champions three straight years. They routinely would sell only half the tickets in their arena. To make things worse, the other team in Madrid—with a much worse record—had larger attendance records than Real Madrid. And both teams played in the same arena.

Yes, it seems logical that if you win, you will draw fans. But that premise is just as wrong as the one that says the best product gets the biggest market share.

- **A curse on your product.** This is an interesting wrinkle. The Nets did have a curse on them. *The Curse of Dr. J.* The Nets won two championships in the old ABA. However, upon entering the NBA, they were extremely undercapitalized. The solution: they *sold* Julius Erving—Dr. J—the most exciting player in the history of the game until Michael Jorden came along, to the

Philadelphia 76ers. Picture the Chicago Bulls selling Michael Jordan for *cash*. How would the Bulls fans in Chicago react? Ever since the Nets sold Dr. J, they have been consistently lousy. From championships to lousy, that's *The Curse of Dr. J.*

- **Not even the most popular product in a company-owned store.** The Nets weren't the most popular pro basketball team in their own market. This is like having a company-owned store where you can really promote your own product and give it favorable aisle positioning, but your prime competitor *still* beats you.

  The Knicks have been an institution in the New York, northern New Jersey, southern Connecticut area. People were born and raised to be Knicks fans. The Knicks are more popular than the Nets in New Jersey. You can see this every time the Knicks come across the Hudson River to play the Nets. Playing against the Nets in New Jersey, the Knicks have the home court advantage. In one game, the crowd filled the arena with the chant of DE-FENSE, DE-FENSE when the Nets were staging a comeback. After being with the Portland Trail Blazers for eleven years, I had never seen anything like it.

- **Customers lacking identity in themselves.** This is an unusual characteristic for customers of a product to have. Well, the Nets had it. There was a lack of state identity in New Jersey. I'll explain.

  In most states, the residents identify with the largest city in the state. That city's newspapers and TV stations are considered the de facto voice of the state. Not in New Jersey. The largest city in New Jersey is Newark. Residents of New Jersey don't even want to admit that Newark is in the state, let alone identify with it.

Besides not recognizing that there is indeed a Newark, residents of New Jersey are fed daily megadoses of New York media. The major TV and radio stations are from New York City. New Jersey does have two major newspapers (New York has four), but the sports pages are New York–oriented. The two cable sports channels are New York sports channels.

To compound the problem, residents of New York view New Jersey as they would Sioux City, Iowa, or Edmonton, Canada. With that vision, why would any New Yorker go to Sioux City, Iowa, to watch a sporting event? Why would any New Yorker go to New Jersey to see the Nets play? Maybe to see the Knicks play a road game.

- **Controversial ownership.** With most products or companies, the owners are nameless and faceless to the public. Not in sports. The Nets' seven owners were dubbed the "Secaucus Seven" by the newspapers. Since you're now an owner, I guess we would have to change the nickname. Secaucus Eight? That's not quite as snappy, but we'll go with it for the moment.

    You won't like how you and your fellow owners are portrayed in the media. Stumbling. Bumbling. You're characters who would get lost if you tried to walk around the block. In reality, the Secausus Seven (and I assume you, too) were nice guys—bright, personally successful, and well-intentioned. Their problem wasn't themselves, it was the structure of their ownership. There wasn't a managing partner, so they divvied up responsibility within the club. One owner would dabble in player personnel, another in marketing, another in finance, etc. As a result, there were seven different voices, seven different visions trying to run the team. With you joining the ownership group, there would be eight. You'll find the decision-making lethargic at best.

PULL OUT THE WAX AND CRASH ON THE ROCKS?

After reading the above about the Nets, and if you're still pretending to be Ulysses, you now might want to yank the wax out of your crew's ears and crash into the rocks. However, if you choose to sail on, think about what you have to do to market the New Jersey Nets.

Here's what we came up with.

1: What was our market? Northern New Jersey would be the target market. By itself, New Jersey is a terrific market. To put it into perspective, if you lifted northern New Jersey up and placed it in the middle of Nebraska, it would be the eighth largest market in the United States. New Jersey isn't as glamorous or as high profile as New York City, but it is big and prosperous. Believe me, if you're a pro sports team, you can operate well in the eighth largest market in the country.

Sure, Manhattan is a terrific lure, but Manhattan wasn't needed to successfully market this hapless team.

Identifying a Market Where You Can Win

The Ulysses method. Many times, marketers of unsuccessful products get lured to marketing a market or market segment where they can't win. But the market is so alluring, so enticing. What happens is that they end up crashing on the rocks. Instead of crashing on the rocks and dying, put some wax in your crew's ears. Better yet, put wax in your own ears. You don't really need to hear that siren song.

Herman's Sporting Goods got lured into thinking they could develop into a national chain. They spent a fortune expanding into every market they looked at. I'm sure they ran some pretty projections of what a national chain of sporting goods stores could deliver. They should have put wax in their ears. Herman's has emerged from Chapter 11 bankruptcy with stores in only three East Coast states.

2: How would we market our product? We would not market the Nets as the traditional hometown team. How can you market a team to a hometown that doesn't recognize that they are the hometown? And even if they did recognize that they were the hometown, no hometown would identify with such a sorry team. Trying to market to a hometown was one of the mistakes that the Nets had been making.

We were going to forget the hometown concept like we forgot Manhattan. If the *Guinness Book of World Records* recorded such a category, the Nets would probably be the first team to ever *not* recognize their hometown. If you won't market to Manhattan, and you choose not to market your hometown, who do you market to?

The hometown.

But we weren't going to market the Nets. We were going to market the *opponents*. While that may sound really strange, aren't the opponents an attribute of our product?

Look at attributes that other teams might have that the Nets didn't have:

Product Attribute	Most Teams	Nets
Competitive team	Yes	No
Hope for a competitive team	Yes	No*
Hometown support	Yes	No
Popular players	Yes	No**
No curses	Yes	The Curse of Dr. J

*How can I say no hope? Actually, there was hope, but the tradition of the Nets was hopeless teams. It's impossible to change that mind-set with talk.

**In 1995 the Nets' Derrick Coleman was the cover boy on *Sports Illustrated*. However, he was featured as the NBA's biggest crybaby.

In the case of the Nets, we weren't going to market players that were losers. We were going to market Michael Jordan, Shaq, Charles Barkley, and Patrick Ewing. If you wanted to see these marquee players, you really couldn't get a ticket at Madison Square Garden unless you paid a fortune to a scalper. But you could see these players in New Jersey. Sure, you had to watch them play against the Nets, but these players had to play against somebody.

There's Something Good in Every Product, I Think

What attribute of your product can give you something to market? If you've got a product or company that needs jump-starting, you're probably marketing the wrong attribute.

We've taken a look at the Nets. All the natural attributes that are usually available for a pro sports team weren't there for the Nets. So instead of trying to take those attributes that weren't there and ram them down the customers' throats, we picked an attribute that was there—the attraction of the marquee players on the opposing teams.

Does this work for other products? Sure it does. You can look at cars, air travel, and hamburgers to see examples of picking the only attribute a product has and running with it.

For instance, in the 1960s and 1970s Burger King was seriously challenging McDonald's. McDonald's had more stores, a larger advertising budget, better fries, cleaner stores, Ronald McDonald, and kids. McDonald's had *everything*, and Burger King had only two attributes to market: the Whopper was bigger than the Big Mac and their burgers were broiled, not fried like McDonald's. If you looked for other attributes, you really couldn't find any. Those two attributes, however, were powerful, and they made Burger King a solid number two in the fast-food business. But then Burger King heard the sirens' song.

The sirens' song was sung by *kids.* Instead of staying with the two attributes it had and running with them forever, Burger King decided to market to *kids.* Do kids care if their burger is broiled or fried? Of course not. Do they care that the Whopper is bigger? If anything, their hands are too small to eat a Whopper without getting it all over them. McDonald's *owned* the kids of America. The only way that Burger King could lure the kids away from McDonald's would be through the parents—the bigger eaters who liked a bigger sandwich that was grilled, not fried. These parents would drag their kids to Burger King and load them up with a Junior Whopper.

Burger King didn't put wax in their ears. They listened to the siren's song. They crashed on the rocks. They almost died.

Once you get an attribute that works, why would you ever give it up?

3: What would we focus on? We would focus on family entertainment. Every pro sports team needs big corporations to purchase season tickets. If you went to a Knicks game, you would be enveloped by a crowd of dark blue pinstripe suits. Want to know what fat-cat corporate America looks like? Go to a Knicks game. This corporate participation has a long history. It was a tradition in New York to leave work, throw down a couple of drinks, then cab it to Madison Square Garden and catch the Knicks.

The corporate culture in most major markets includes season tickets to a pro sports team. These corporations use their tickets for client entertaining or for their employees. It wasn't that way in New Jersey. Not that way at all.

We got a list of the top two hundred corporations in northern New Jersey and cross-checked it with our season ticket holder list. Of those two hundred top corporations, only twelve had season tickets with the Nets. I don't know what the numbers were for the Knicks, but the reverse could be true—probably less than twelve of the top two hundred corporations in New York City did not have Knicks season tickets.

We set up a sales staff to improve our numbers with corporations, but essentially we took our marketing to the people, to the fans and families. Part of that was positioning the Nets games as family entertainment.

If you wore a dark blue pinstriped suit, we'd allow you to come to our game. After all, dark blue pinstriped suits are people, too. They aren't all cold, cut-throat businessmen. They have even been known to have families. Our focus was clearly on family entertainment, and that's how we wanted to differentiate ourselves.

NOW WE KNOW WHO IN ALL BILLY HELL WE ARE, DO YOU?

This chapter may seem a little silly to you. After all, every company knows who they are, right? Wrong. Even the mega-companies can lose their identity along the way. How about General Motors? They bought Hughes Aircraft and Ross Perot's company, EDP. Roger Smith, GM's chairman at the time, seemed to be fashioning General Motors as more of a holding company than a company that builds cars and trucks. The car and truck business suffered.

Any business is lured by sirens, and under the spell of the siren song, any company can lose the focus of what they are and who their market is. This doesn't mean that companies can't try other things. Sure they can, but in a controlled way that is isolated from the regular day-to-day business.

With the Nets, we were finally getting down to what we were. In the process, we determined what we weren't. We weren't the Knicks. We weren't a favorite of the hometown. We weren't for Manhattanites. We weren't for fat-cat big corporations. Here's what we were:

1. Our target market was northern New Jersey.
2. Our target audience was people who wanted to see the stars of the NBA.
3. We would market as fan friendly and family friendly.

Now that we knew who we were, we had to market ourselves. And market we did.

In four seasons, our attendance jumped up from dead last (twenty-seventh) to twelfth. The increase in attendance automatically helped goose revenue in other areas like hot dogs, beer, parking, and, importantly, local sponsorships. Because more people were going to Nets games, a sponsorship for a local company became more realistic. In four years, the Nets local sponsorship revenues increased from $400,000 to over $7 million.

As an owner of the Nets, you enjoyed this growth. Sure, the team wasn't any better, but at least your investment was growing. Four years before, *Financial World* magazine estimated the sale value of the Nets at $52 million. After using Ulysses as a model, the value of the franchise went up to $92 million. Not bad for just putting some wax in your ears, huh?

THE QUICK-FIX SILVER BULLET

The New Jersey Nets became a great acid test for marketing ideas. If it would work for the Nets, it would work for *any* prod-

marketing ideas worked better than others. One is
e "quick-fix silver bullet." That's in the next chapter.
turn to the next chapter, though, you have a little
_. It shouldn't take long. Just fill out the following test.

A Simple Test You Can Take

(Fill in the blank.) **For which market(s) should I put
wax in my crew's ears (and my own ears)?**

_____

(Fill in the blank.) **Which market out there is where I
have the best chance to succeed?**

_____

(Fill in the blank.) **Which product attributes can't I use
in marketing my product?**

    A. _____

    B. _____

    C. _____

(Fill in the blank.) **Which product attribute can I best
use to help jump-start my product or company?**

_____

Answers

1. There is probably a market out there that you're trying to
get into. I'm not talking about a little experiment, I'm talking

about where you're throwing money and manpower into the equation. Is that market a potential siren? Will you and your crew hear this terrific song and crash into the rocks?

2. If you have the best chance to succeed in this market, why not throw more money and manpower into it? Why not make it a bigger success?

3. Sometimes a bad attribute can be used as a good one. *Listerine, the taste you hate twice a day.* In most cases, if you try touting a bad attribute as a good one, your product and company lose credibility. It would be like promoting the Nets as the best team in basketball. *Nobody* would believe that, and any positive attributes that we had would also be disbelieved. Every product has some bad attributes. Don't try to fool the customer by hyping a bad attribute.

4. A lot of times, you only need one product attribute to make it work. What is that one product attribute of yours that is better than all the others? What is the second best? Run with those.

We did that with the Nets. To give you an idea of where we had come from, let's look at Michael Jordan, the greatest gate attraction ever. In the 1991–92 season, the Bulls were on their way to winning their second straight NBA championship. During that season, Michael Jordan played in 102 games, including playoffs. Of those 102 games, 100 of them were sell-outs. The two that didn't sell out? You guessed it—they were against the Nets at Meadowlands Arena. In fact, the Nets didn't sell out one game that year, let alone any games during the previous four years. However, by packaging Michael Jordan with Larry Bird and Magic Johnson, we made a ticket package that was bigger than it actually was.

The next season we started to sell out Meadowlands Arena through ticket packages. Five times. That was probably the

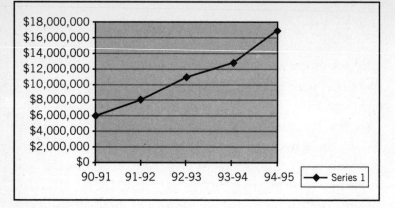

most difficult marketing effort I've ever been involved with. The following year, we sold out twelve times, then nineteen, then twenty-two, and at the time of this writing, the Nets were scheduled to sell out the arena thirty-five times.

The increase in attendance and the increase of sellouts translated, of course, to dollars. Using the principles in jump-start marketing, the Nets' ticket revenue went from $5 million to almost $17 million in four years.

3. A QUICK-FIX SILVER BULLET

Ground rule #3: Increase the frequency of purchases by your customers.

You don't see it much any more because most of the major pro sports teams travel either by their own airplane or charter. Just a few years ago, NBA teams would travel commercial—they would wander through airports just like you and me.

During that era, there was always one thing that was consistent with each team. While waiting for the plane, at least one player would scour the area for a newspaper that was left behind by another traveler. It wasn't that the players couldn't afford a newspaper. They weren't making several million dollars a year like many are now, but the average pay was almost $500,000 per year.

When a player would search the waiting area, invariably you would see and overhear something like this: A wandering player would pick up a discarded *Wall Street Journal* and flip it open. Another player sitting nearby would say, "Forget it, somebody already got the sports section."

Players, of course, have always been cheap. Besides trying to encourage you to buy a newspaper—one that has a sports section—they're the best at conning a meal out of you.

Every free meal to them is money saved on their per diem. When the team is traveling, players now receive $80 a day for food. They get this money at the beginning of a road trip. If the team will be traveling for seven days, each player receives $560. Cash. Even though they earn millions, this seems like a lot of cash to them. Their paychecks are usually sent to their agents or financial advisors. The agents pay all the bills and give the players an allowance.

This fixation on per diem doesn't end when a player's career is over. For instance, this fixation stayed with Pat Riley long after his nine-year playing career ended. Riley turned out to be the best coach in the history of the NBA. Sure, you might say that Red Auerbach was, but Red won all those titles *before* player free agency. Riley ended up in first place in his division the first ten years that he coached in the NBA.

When he signed the most lucrative deal in the history of coaching with the Miami Heat, he received a reported $30 million deal, which included some ownership of the team. His titles are president and coach. And he negotiated $300 per day of per diem for food to go along with that $30 million. Riley's per diem was almost four times what any other coach in the NBA received.

One thing he doesn't have to dip into his $300 per day per diem for is newspapers. Newspapers—with sports sections—are distributed free on the charter flights.

■

Wouldn't it be great if there was a quick-fix silver bullet?
Well, there is.
That's the good news.
The bad news? Not everybody can use it, at least right away.

WHO CAN USE THE QUICK-FIX
SILVER BULLET RIGHT AWAY

Suppose for a moment that you know who in all Billy Hell you are. Now that you know, you want to increase your sales with a quick-fix silver bullet. Do you:

A. Run a big TV advertising campaign.

B. Run a full-page newspaper ad.

C. Buy some lists and send out thousands of brochures.

D. Take the Yellow Pages and/or White Pages and call everyone to tell them about your product.

E. All of the above.

F. None of the above.

The answer is (F), none of the above.

The answer is this: *You personally ask each of your present customers on a one-to-one basis to buy some more.*

This is worth repeating.

You personally ask each of your present customers on a one-to-one basis to buy some more.

You'll be able to use this quick-fix silver bullet right now if you know the names, addresses, and phone numbers of your customers. If you don't, don't feel bad. There are plenty of companies that are in the same situation—they don't know the names of their customers. If you don't know the names, addresses, and phone numbers of your customers, start getting that information so that you can use the now semi-quick-fix silver bullet.

YOU'VE SEEN THIS FISH BOWL

You've probably been in a restaurant where they have a fish bowl near the cash register. Customers can drop their business cards in the fish bowl for a chance at a free lunch. At these restaurants, I always ask the cashier what they do with the business cards that don't win. They usually shrug or say that after they pick a winner, they throw the rest of the cards out.

Let's think about this for a moment. What if the restaurant owner sent a letter *the same day* to each person that dropped a business card into the fish bowl? The letter could thank them for their patronage and invite them back. If they came back within ten days and mentioned the letter to the waitress, they would receive a free dessert or free cup of coffee.

Do you think that would be effective in building that restaurant's business? You better believe it! What if a once-every-two-weeks customer appreciated the letter, appreciated the nice gesture of free dessert or free coffee, and came back a little more frequently? Like once a week. The restaurant would increase its business in geometric progression. The restaurant could significantly increase its business just from the people that have found the restaurant on their own. Using this quick-fix silver bullet, a restaurant would probably become a Yogi Berra restaurant. You know, "Nobody goes there anymore, it's too crowded."

Increasing the frequency of purchase by customers is the best and most efficient way of building a business. It is a quick-fix silver bullet.

SHOOTING THE SILVER BULLET

A few years ago, a friend of mine had an all-too-typical problem with his business. He manufactured these crazy devices that find money in the sand. You've probably seen the product if you've spent any time at the beach. There's a twelve-inch disc on the end of a pole about the length of a golf club. Attached to the pole is a small metal detector. At the top of the pole are meters that tell you if there is some small fortune below your feet.

My friend had a new improved version of his product, but he couldn't afford to advertise it or fill the pipelines in stores. The bank wouldn't give him a loan to do those two things. Over a beer, he asked me if I had any suggestions.

"Do you have the names and addresses of any of the people that have purchased your products?" I asked.

"No," he said. "People purchase their products at retail stores. I doubt if the stores have their names."

He took a sip from his beer, thinking. He took another bigger sip. "Wait a minute," he said, looking as if he should have said eureka. "I've got boxes and boxes of warranties sent in by people that have bought my product. They're just in boxes—I never even look at them because our product never breaks down. But each one has the buyer's name, address, and phone number."

"*Eureka!*" I said.

There were about 5,000 names. These people had already indicated that they were interested in my friend's product— they had *purchased* one. There would be a certain portion of those people who would be interested in the latest upgrade. It would cost about $1,500 in postage to find out who those people were. There would be no out-of-pocket cost for letterhead and envelopes, because they had already been paid for.

"What would a person pay for one of these fortune finders?" I asked.

"Nine hundred dollars," he said. (I thought, A person will have to find an awful lot of nickels, quarters, and rare old pennies to make this investment pay off.)

"How much do they cost to make and how much out-of-pocket money will it take?"

"They cost about $150 each to make," my friend said. "I've got enough material in inventory from other products that I could make about one hundred units. I could sell them through the distributors to the stores, but I wouldn't get my money for sixty to ninety days."

"So," I said, "at least for the short term, these new products don't cost you any out-of-pocket money."

He nodded, finished his beer, and ordered another round.

I did some math on a paper napkin.

I wrote down $900.

I then wrote down 100 underneath it with an X in front of it. That represented the number of buyers that I thought my friend could get from a mailing. Remember, this was not a mailing to the general public. If it was a mailing to the general public, you wouldn't find 1 person in 1,000 or even 100,000 that would be interested in this product. This was a mailing to his *satisfied* customers. This was a mailing to people who had already shown a serious interest in finding a buried fortune in their backyard or on the beach by buying this product in the past.

I then multiplied the two numbers.

$$\begin{array}{r} \$900 \\ \underline{\times\ 100} \\ \$90{,}000 \end{array}$$

I showed him the napkin. "Would that give you the financing to fill the pipelines?"

He was stunned.

"From your mailing to your existing customers, my feeling is that you would sell more than one hundred units. You'd probably sell five hundred. How fast can you buy the material to make these gadgets?"

"With cash, not long," he said. "A week."

I wrote some new numbers down on the paper napkin. This time I multiplied the price of the gadget ($900) by the additional sales from the mailing (400).

$$\begin{array}{r} \$900 \\ \times\ 400 \\ \hline \$360,000 \end{array}$$

"You're going to find out what just-in-time delivery really means with your suppliers. You'll be getting orders—and *cash* with each order—and you'll need to keep your supplies rolling in."

Now I wrote down the totals from my two math exercises.

$$\begin{array}{r} \$90,000 \\ +\ \$360,000 \\ \hline \$450,000 \end{array}$$

My friend just stared at the napkin. After a minute of thinking about those numbers, the stunned feeling started to wear off. He had spotted a problem. "If I go direct to my customers, I could lose my distributors and retailers. I'd be undercutting their sales by going direct."

I told him that I felt he would be "seeding the market" with this direct approach. It would help build awareness for the dealers. But if it made him feel better, I suggested, he could cut the dealers and distributors in on it. Give the dealers 10 percent of all sales that originate from the zip codes of where their stores were. Give the distributor 5 percent. It would be like money from heaven to them.

If my figures on the napkin were correct, the dealers and distributors would receive $67,500 for doing nothing! The stores and the distributors would be making money without risking anything in inventory. There would be one caveat: The money that was to be given to the dealers would not be cash, but credits for future orders for this hot new product.

We worked on a mailing. Since he didn't have the budget to produce a slick, glossy brochure, we did a four-page letter from him, the president of the company, to each one of his known customers. I had him sign each of the 5,000 letters.

The letter was simple. My friend wrote about a major break-through in his technology. He was offering this product first to his loyal customers before he offered them to the general public through retail stores.

The response came in at a little over 10 percent. With an influx of cash and a hit product on his hands, my friend then sold his company.

BUILDING A SILVER BULLET ARSENAL IN NEW JERSEY

A couple of weeks after that dinner with the New Jersey Nets owners, we had cut a deal. I would consult for the Nets. On my first day in the Nets office, I wanted to look good and employ the quick-fix silver bullet.

This is what I found:

- **The Nets were great at saving hard-drive space on their computers.** The Nets had the names of their current season ticket holders on computer. That was good.

The Nets didn't have the names of last year's season ticket holders. Or the year before last. That wasn't so good.

"We wipe them from the computer each year to save disk space," I was told. Since the Nets only renewed about 70 percent of their season ticket holders each year, there were about 30 percent of their previous buyers that could be candidates for the quick-fix silver bullet.

Disk space is, of course, very cheap. Getting names of qualified buyers is very expensive. In the Nets case, 30 percent of their qualified buyers were wiped from the computer bank. Even though these now gone-forever buyers were not satisfied customers (they didn't renew), they would have been ideal candidates for a special ticket package that featured just the marquee players in the NBA.

- **Throwing away names of future customers.** One of the great things about pro sports is that you have fans (potential ticket-buying customers) who will clearly show interest in your product. One way is that they will call you up and ask for a schedule of games. Very few businesses have this type of a situation, where thousands of potential buyers will search out the company and identify themselves as potential buyers.

  The Nets dutifully handled these requests. They would have student interns write (by hand) the fan's name and address on an envelope, put the schedule in the envelope, and mail it.

  There were thousands of fans who wanted the schedule. Of those thousands, no names and addresses were kept. There was no quick-fix silver bullet aimed at them.

- **Hear-No-Name, See-No-Name mentality.** When a person uses a credit card to buy tickets over the phone from TicketMaster, that person gives their name and mailing address. TicketMaster then mails the tickets.

These are great names. After all, these people have identified themselves as being interested in a specific event, whether it be a Bruce Springsteen concert, a Barbra Streisand concert, or even a New Jersey Nets game. They've also identified themselves as willing to pay a premium for their tickets, because TicketMaster tacks on a $4–$6 service charge. Because the Nets use the TicketMaster system, TicketMaster will download those names from their computer to the Nets computer. If you want. The Nets didn't want.

In fact, the Nets culture was to *not* keep names. All names that they kept were current season ticket holders. If these people did not renew their season tickets, it was like Communist Russia—they were wiped from the history books.

THE SEMI-QUICK-FIX SILVER BULLET

I started in May, 1991, as a consultant to the New Jersey Nets. This was playoff time for sixteen of the NBA's twenty-seven teams. The Nets won twenty-six of their eighty-two games, and thus their season was over. However, even before this dismal season had ended, we had revved up another season, the selling season.

We install a sales staff to call on New Jersey corporations (see chapter 18). Just as important, we started to build a database of known Nets fans.

Where did we start?

- **We re-created some history.** After a season, TicketMaster would wipe their computer files clean. But they took a precaution. They would store each year's files for five years on tape in an archive. We had them retrieve those tapes and transfer the Nets season ticket holder names and addresses to us. Since TicketMaster's computer couldn't mix and match from one year to the next, and the Nets were woefully short of computers, we did it the old-fashioned way: We got those interns to do it by hand. The Nets had taken a very bold first step toward increasing their sales—they had started a list of qualified buyers from people who had not renewed their season tickets. Why were the names of people that did not renew good names? Here's why:

A. *Things change.* Maybe they couldn't afford full forty-one-game season tickets anymore. A fourteen-game ticket package might be perfect for them.

B. *We know they were once interested in our product.* They might not be interested in the Nets because of the consistently lousy team, but they would probably still be interested in what we thought our product was—NBA opponents with superstars like Michael Jordan, Shaq, etc.

C. *They knew how to get to the arena.* Many times, a business will take its location for granted. After all, employees seem to find their way each day. However, people who are visiting a business for the first time are a bit intimidated. That intimidation could lead to them not coming at all.

• **Re-creating even more history.** We had TicketMaster search their computer for the names of Nets ticket buyers who used their credit cards for a purchase of tickets to one game over the phone. There were thousands of names. The typical one-game buyer will go to three games a season. We felt that we could target a mailing to them to increase their frequency of attendance just a little bit to five or even seven games. Increasing the frequency of attendance of these "one-gamers" would contribute hundreds of thousands of dollars in increased sales in the future.

- **No name gets tossed.** One of the reasons that the Nets wrote the names and addresses on envelopes by hand was that there were only four computers in the office. One was for the executive secretary, one was for the other executive secretary, one was for the ticket office, and one was for the accounting department.

  One of my first orders as a consultant wasn't an order to increase revenue, but to buy some computers. We bought four. (Two years later, when I joined the Nets full-time, we placed a computer on every desk to bring the total to over forty.)

  When fans called in for a schedule card, the Nets staff now typed them into a computer database. The fans would still get the schedule cards they wanted. The Nets would get the name and address of a person who was at least interested enough in the Nets to want to know when the games were played.

  We started to develop a mentality that we would capture every name. In fact, I gave the Nets staff an impossible goal. I wanted us to get the name, address, and daytime and night-time phone number of *everybody* who purchased a ticket to a Nets game in the coming year: man, woman, child, or Knicks fan. Sure, we wouldn't get all the names, but why not try for it?

  At the same time, I gave the staff another impossible challenge. I wanted us to get the name, address, and daytime and nighttime phone number of every Nets and NBA fan, whether they went to Nets games or not. We scoured northern New Jersey. To give you an idea of how extensive our search was, we even tapped fan mail from kids.

If a kid wrote a letter to one of the players, the public relations department usually handled it. However, now that kid's name went into the computer. We were developing a list of "To the Parents of . . . "

This fixation on names led to a list of over 75,000 names of people who had qualified themselves in some way as having an interest in the Nets. While it wasn't a quick-fix silver bullet, these names would pay huge dividends for years to come.

For instance, we would send a ticket catalog to these names. The catalog was a full-color, eight-page booklet. On each page we featured a different ticket product. We would feature a seven-game package on one page, a special family package to one game on another page. It would cost us about $19,000 to prepare and mail this catalog. From that mailing, we would receive $300,000 in ticket sales. (For more on this, see chapter 11.)

This type of intense fixation on names will serve any business. The more names of people that are interested in your product that you keep, the more effective the quick-fix silver bullet.

A WARNING ABOUT NAMES

A name is not a name is not a name.

For the quick-fix silver bullet to work, you can't just have any name. For the quick-fix silver bullet to work, the names have to be of people who have somehow shown an interest in your product. If they have already shown an interest, then the quick-fix silver bullet is intended to increase their frequency of purchase. Increasing the frequency of purchase will indeed jump-start a company.

You might think that you can just buy a list of people who

have common characteristics that you think would be interested in your product. List-buying does work. But list buying isn't a quick-fix silver bullet. What it will be is an *expense*—an expense to ferret out of those people on the list who are interested in your product. Once these people have been ferreted out, then they become candidates for the quick-fix silver bullet.

HOW SUCCESSFUL WAS THE NETS SEMI-QUICK-FIX SILVER BULLET?

As much as I would have liked to have been an instant hero, we weren't able to use even the semi-quick-fix silver bullet. In trying to jump-start a product or company, not all the tools are going to be available to you. It would have been great if we could have shot the quick-fix silver bullet, but there's a reason that a product or company needs jump-starting. One of the major reasons is that the company doesn't know who its own customers are—by name, address, and phone number. Without the names of customers, I'm not sure that there is a quick-fix silver bullet. We didn't despair, we just worked on the fundamentals of retrieving names, readying ourselves for the delayed quick-fix silver bullet.

THE DELAYED QUICK-FIX SILVER BULLET

One of the first payouts from our new lists was a delayed quick-fix silver bullet aimed at our first natural targets, the existing season ticket holders.

Season ticket holders make a big investment in pro basketball. Four season tickets to Nets games cost $8,000. Four season tickets to Knicks games cost $16,000. You'd think with these types of investments that the fan would have spent enough money on pro basketball for the year. You'd think wrong.

On a forty-one-game home schedule, some games are bigger than others. Even fewer games are *monster* games. These games feature opponents with marquee players like Michael Jordan, The Shaq, and Hakeem Olajuwon. Other monster games for the Nets would be the "home" games against the Knicks at Meadowlands Arena. For these games, a season ticket buyer would need more tickets for business associates, family, or friends.

After the season ticket holder had renewed, we sent them a letter about how to buy *more* tickets. These weren't tickets to our lesser attractions—those they couldn't give away—but tickets to our best games. We had put together a five-game "Monster Game Ticket Package" for season ticket holders. Were the season ticket holders of the hapless Nets willing to spend even more money on tickets?

Let's look at the math.

We had only about eight hundred season ticket accounts when we first mailed the letter. Postage was cheaper then (isn't it always), so our out-of-pocket expense was only twenty-eight cents each.

Each five-game Monster Game Ticket Package was priced at $200 each. We sold a ton of them! Over $100,000 worth.

$100,000 revenue from Monster Games
- $224 postage costs
$99,776 profit from mailing

You might say, "Hey, you would have sold out those games anyway."

Are you sure? After all, this is the New Jersey Nets.

In chapter 2, I wrote about how the Nets went from zero sellouts to five in the first year of my consulting. Guess which five games sold out? Having season ticket holders buy additional tickets to the monster games was absolutely instrumental in selling those games out. The delayed quick-fix silver bullet helped us get an easy victory and build some marketing confidence in a market where easy victories were rare.

QUICK-FIX SILVER BULLET USED ALL THE TIME

After reading this, the thought probably struck you that you could use the quick-fix silver bullet for more than just a quick fix. You're exactly right.

By knowing the names, addresses, and phone numbers of your customers and people that are interested in your product, you can use the quick-fix silver bullet all the time.

Once we built our database at the Nets, we fired the quick-fix silver bullet all the time. In one instance, the quick-fix silver bullet was our ticket catalog. This was a similar format to the Land's End catalog, except we didn't feature clothing, but different ticket packages. As previously mentioned in this chapter, the response was terrific—$300,000 of revenue to just $19,000 in expenses. Why not shoot that bullet more frequently? We did. The next year we added some more names and sent out two catalogs. The second catalog did as well as the first. The third year we sent out *four* ticket catalogs. That year, we ended up spending about $100,000 in preparing, printing, and mailing ticket catalogs to people who had somehow indicated they were interested in us. That same year, we received about $900,000 in sales from those catalogs. The only reason we didn't send them out more frequently is that our season was only six months long. Toward the last third of the season, there are fewer and fewer games to feature in our packages.

So once you have developed a culture for collecting names of people who are interested in your product, fire away. Again and again.

A Simple Test You Can Take

(True or False.) **I vow not to be like the restaurant and just toss away the names of my customers.**

True   False

(Fill in the blank.) **In one simple sentence, write down what the quick-fix silver bullet is.**

_____

(Fill in the blank.) **How can I best deploy the quick-fix silver bullet?**

_____

Answers

1: True. During the question-and-answer portion of speeches where I've featured the quick-fix silver bullet, I'll invariably get the questions:

Q: "I can see where the quick-fix silver bullet works for tickets, but not for high-ticket items that cost $25,000 to $100,000 or even more."

A: I usually answer, "Wrong. It works with high-ticket items that aren't purchased as frequently." I then give an example. That example is in the next chapter.

Q: "We know the names of our customers—they are distributors. The quick-fix silver bullet wouldn't work with them."

A: This is like my friend with the metal detector. You can find a fortune in the sand. He thought he didn't know who the final user of his product was. But he had the warranties sitting in boxes. With other companies, getting the name of the final user of the product may be more difficult. I have a few ideas on that, also in the next chapter.

Q: "We make batteries and we only have three customers—the car companies. We sure know their names. So how do we use the quick-fix silver bullet?"

A: This person probably can't. Most likely, "New Customers from Heaven" (chapter 5) would be more appropriate.

It's easy to dismiss the concept of the quick-fix silver bullet as "that won't work with my product" or "that won't work in my market." Unfortunately, that's a typical stance when faced with a different idea. In many cases, it takes work to get the names of people who have somehow shown an interest in your product. But getting the names is the hard part. Cashing in on those names with big jump-start sales is the easy part. Without the hard part, however, there is no easy part, no quick-fix silver bullet.

2: The quick-fix silver bullet is: Increasing the frequency of purchases by your customers.

3: Don't just skip this question and move on to the next chapter. You have the answer to this one. Take a few moments and write down how you would employ the quick-fix silver bullet. Right here. Right now.

_____

_____

_____

_____

_____

If you've jotted down *something* here, you're on the right track and you've answered the question correctly. Now just take what you've written, flesh it out, and run with it.

4. AH SO DESU (IT IS SO, IT IS SO.)

Ground rule #4: Get the name and address of the end user of your product.

The New Jersey Nets were generally regarded as the ninth most popular pro sports team in the New York metropolitan market. There are nine pro teams in that market. I might be able to dispute that, but the most I could nudge the Nets up in the rankings would be to eighth.

We knew we had a challenge in marketing sponsorships for the Nets. One strategy we had was to work our terrain. In our terrain, you would quickly notice that there are a large number of Japanese companies based there.

I hired a young Japanese man to become our international director of marketing. Yoshi Okamoto became the first international director of marketing for any pro team.

We didn't just call on the American divisions of these Japanese companies. We felt that we had to tell our story to the home offices in Japan. The reason was simple. Many large expenditures need final approval in Japan. We felt that a no-name team like the Nets might not get that approval, even if we were able to get the American division to recommend us.

So Yoshi and I traveled to Japan twice a year. We didn't sell specific sponsorship packages, we were just trying to establish recognition for the New Jersey Nets.

In two years, we went from having one Japanese/American company as a sponsor to twelve. Along the way, I made some personal friendships that I value highly.

On one of our trips, we were having lunch with a large company that owned a team in the Japan Basketball League. At one point, the general manager of the team asked me if I could recommend an American to be their head coach. A *gai-jin* (foreigner) had never been a head coach in the league.

When I got back to the United States, I thought of several candidates. I didn't take this lightly. The wrong candidate could be very embarrassing for the company and could bury me in the process.

Besides having all of the qualifications of a coach, I knew that my candidate would have to have the desire to live in a different culture. This would eliminate many candidates. However, I did have the perfect candidate: Jack Schalow. He had been an assistant coach while I was with the Portland Trail Blazers.

Besides his ten years' experience in the NBA, Jack had coached in college and had been a head coach in the CBA. Above all, he was a teacher of the game. He was tired of "baby-sitting" players in the NBA. He wanted to coach.

There were a couple of problems, though.

Jack didn't smoke or drink. Jack didn't eat meat; he loved eating pounds of fruit. You'd think that those were admirable qualities, and they are. But much socializing with Japanese businessmen is done over drinks in smoke-filled bars. Besides not smoking, Jack was *allergic* to smoke.

I explained this to my Japanese friends. They said no problem. They wanted a coach, whether he smoked or drank or not.

The general manager came to the United States and we all had dinner in New York City. A deal was cut. A couple of months later, the company made the announcement to the Japanese press. I was invited to sit alongside Jack at the press conference. Before we went to the press conference, we stopped in a small food market in the New Otani Hotel. Jack picked up a cantaloupe. "This is my favorite fruit," he said. "What's this cost in American money," he asked, pointing to the yen price tag.

I did some quick math in my head. It has to be wrong, I thought. I did the math again.

"One hundred dollars," I said.

I thought I had lost Jack right there. But I knew that the company would be able to provide Jack with fresh fruit—without the price tags.

Jack worked out marvelously. The Japanese team had been a perennial loser. Now they were winners. Jack was named coach of the year and signed a three-year extension to his contract. Jack had adapted to a marvelous diet of fruit, rice, and cereal.

On occasion, I thought, Jack probably ate $400 breakfasts. If only Pat Riley knew that another coach, in Japan no less, was getting more per diem for breakfast alone.

■

I was on a private island—just a forty-minute boat ride from mainland Japan—and the quick-fix silver bullet became a topic of conversation. We had started the day seeing a Japan Basketball League game. I had come over to see the game with a team that we had developed a "sister" relationship with two years before. Unlike in the United States, teams in Japan are owned by big corporations. In this case, the team in the Japan Basketball League was owned by a worldwide automotive manufacturer.

We arrived on the island on an early Sunday evening. After taking a bath from the natural hot springs, we met for dinner and drinks.

One of the car executives asked me about my book they knew I was working on. He asked, "Could any of the principles of jump-start marketing that work for selling tickets work in helping us increase our car sales worldwide?"

Even though a basketball ticket would cost about $50 and a new car about $25,000, I said, "Yes. Definitely."

He asked if I could explain one principle.

Between broken Japanese (me) and broken English (them) I brought up the quick-fix silver bullet. I didn't use that moniker, because I wasn't sure how it translated. However, here is the gist of my explanation:

One key principle of jump-start marketing is that you know the name of the final user of your product. You know the names of your primary customers—the dealers—but you don't know the name of the end user, the person that buys the car.

They nodded and agreed. The car dealer knew the name of the buyer. The car manufacturer did not. By not knowing that name, they were risking the fact that the dealer knew how to maximize the sale from that customer.

They nodded and agreed again.

The dealer would try to increase sales from that customer by sending reminder post cards for service, but the manufacturer didn't get any of that service money.

They nodded and agreed. We poured another round of sake.

However, if the dealer tried just a couple of things, the dealer could sell a lot more cars for the manufacturer.

"Please explain, Jon-*san*," they said.

1: Selling a second car to the buyer. Most American families have at least two cars. While they have two or more cars, they usually don't purchase two or three brand-new cars *at the same time*. The purchases are staggered over two or three years or more.

The dealer and the manufacturer should start thinking about selling a *second car* to that family while the ink is drying on the paperwork for the first sale. This wouldn't be the hammer-and-tong sales approach. Some patience and information is needed here.

Instead of just dumping the paperwork in a filing cabinet, the dealer should be filling a database on that customer. That database would have all the traditional information like name, address, etc. Also included in the database would be a listing of the number of vehicles that the person owns by make, model, and year.

The marketing of the second car to the family would start about six months after the purchase of the first vehicle. After six months, the buyer should be a happy buyer, because it is a quality car. The dealer would tap into his data that he gathered when the sale had been made six months before. He might find that the second car is a station wagon that is four years old. The dealer would recommend to the customer a test-drive of either a minivan or four-wheel-drive vehicle and, because they are already customers, a special warranty package. A special warranty package would most likely be appealing to the family, because after four years, they are probably getting nickel-and-dimed to death with repair costs.

For each person that responded to such an invitation, the dealer has basically eliminated the competition. The person is coming in because the dealer's idea made sense.

My hosts nodded and said, "*Ah so desu.*" This translates to something like, "Yes, it is so."

"There's another reason to know the end user's name," I said. By now, they were taking notes on napkins.

2: Increase the frequency of purchase by just a few months. Most people usually think about buying a new car about every three years. Before the customer even starts to *think* about buying a new car, the dealer should be taking steps to market that person a new car.

Before we go on, we'll have to make an assumption. The car is a quality car and the customer is a satisfied customer. Since I was talking with a Japanese car company, we'll make that assumption.

The dealer could then invite the satisfied customer to come in and test-drive the latest vehicle, briefly explaining some of the new improvements that really make a difference.

The majority of people who receive that invitation wouldn't, of course, come in and test-drive the new vehicle. But think about those who did. If you increased the frequency of purchasing a car by just a few months, it makes a huge difference in the number of cars sold.

I pulled a sheet of paper from my suit pocket. I needed more space than what a napkin provided. "Here," I said, "let's take a look at some simple math."

I drew the following table on the paper. I then filled in the columns.

People purchasing	Time frame	Cars sold in 5 years	Cars sold in 7.5 years
1,000	2.5 years	2,000	3,000
1,000	3.0 years	1,000	2,000

"*Ah so desu.*"

Even by using this simple math, they saw that a dealership—and manufacturer—could increase their sales by 50 percent from their regular customers.

I told them that in pro sports, we have seen that increasing the fan's *frequency* of attending games has an effect in geometric progression. Why wouldn't the same marketing principle apply in higher-ticket items like automobiles?

LETTING THE COMPETITION WALK IN THE FRONT DOOR

The above are real reasons that a manufacturer should know the name of the end user. If the manufacturer doesn't know those names, then the manufacturer is dependent on the dealer to increase sales to the satisfied customers. Most dealers will be concentrating on the current walk-in-and-kick-the-tires people. Most dealers will wait until the satisfied customer develops an urge to buy a new car. By then, it may be too late. The satisfied customer may just decide to look at one of the other various automotive options in the marketplace. Now the dealer—and the manufacturer—are facing serious competition. The automotive business is a highly competitive business, and if a satisfied customer is allowed to wander from dealership to dealership, chances have increased considerably that the original dealer will *not* make the sale.

"*Ah so desu.* It is so. It is so."

WHY WAIT 2.5 YEARS?

A little bit later in the evening, one of the executives asked me, "Even though we are known to have patience, this seems like a long time to wait to sell that second car."

"Why wait?" I asked. "Why not start tomorrow?"

I could see that he was understanding me.

Dealerships have all the records of buyers from two and a half years ago. They have that information for no other reason than the warranties. If this company wanted to initiate the quick-fix silver bullet right now, they could.

"*Ah so desu.* It is so. It is so."

It's a simple process. The dealer would just retrieve the records from two and a half years ago. A mailing would be prepared and sent (see chapter 11). A portion of the people that received the letter would respond. My feeling is that about 20 percent or more would.

GETTING THE END USERS' NAMES

I know that the quick-fix silver bullet has automatic success in selling tickets, even for the sorry New Jersey Nets. I also know that the quick-fix silver bullet works in selling metal detectors that would find a fortune in the sand. However, if we wouldn't have captured the names of the people who walked up to buy a ticket at the box office, or if my friend wouldn't have stashed his warranties in boxes, then the quick-fix silver bullet couldn't even be loaded in the gun. There are other manufacturers whose primary customers are distributors, dealers, and retail stores, and those manufacturers never learn the names of the end users of their product. The effectiveness of the quick-fix silver bullet then lies with a third party, and that can be a mostly don't-even-see-the-target situation.

For those manufacturers, it should not be too difficult to collect the names of the end users from distributors, dealers, or retail stores. Here is a suggestion:

Bring the dealer in as a partner.

The manufacturer would do all the work in the partnership. The manufacturer's responsibility in the partnership would be to prepare the mailing to the buyer explaining the offer, pay for the cost of the offer, and pay for the printing and postage. The dealer's responsibility in the partnership would be to provide the names. At first blush, that may sound like a lopsided partnership clearly favoring the dealer. Yes, it definitely would look like that.

But let's take a look at what the manufacturer has to gain. The manufacturer would have *all* of his dealers in the partnership being coordinated into a quick-fix silver bullet program. The manufacturer wouldn't have to rely on the inconsistencies of just a handful of dealerships making the program work. The manufacturer would be making the program work consistently from dealer to dealer. The manufacturer would bear the cost of the quick-fix silver bullet, but that manufacturer does have a marketing budget, I presume, and that manufacturer could do the math like I had done on a napkin. Very few marketing programs could eliminate competition in such a way and yield such a tremendous return.

Ah so desu. It is so. It is so.

A Simple Test You Can Take

(Fill in the blanks, if you can.) **Name at least one industry where the quick-fix silver bullet wouldn't work.**

A. _____

B. _____

C. _____

(Fill in the blank.) **Do your own math on how increasing the frequency of the purchase can increase your sales in geometric progression.**

People purchasing   **Time frame**
Items sold in __ years   **Items sold in __ years**

(Fill in the blank.) **Name one reason why a company wouldn't utilize the quick-fix silver bullet.**

_____

_____

Answers

1: This is a difficult question to answer, because any company could easily use the quick-fix silver bullet. However, there are many companies out there where it wouldn't be efficient. Companies that sell low-cost items like a pack of gum wouldn't be great candidates for the quick-fix silver bullet. But if you're a gum executive, or just somebody who likes to solve knotty marketing problems, I wouldn't bet that you couldn't come up with a use for the quick-fix silver bullet.

2: I can't check your math here. But do I really need to? If the numbers look terrific to you, you'd be off to the races right now with the quick-fix silver bullet regardless of what I had to say. So how do the numbers look?

3: I had one friend tell me that the company that used the quick-fix silver bullet would only be cannibalizing future sales from those same customers. I responded, "You're right." I then asked my friend to do some math. "Let's assume for the moment that each customer would buy either now or six months from now. Getting the customers money six months earlier must mean *something*, right? Five percent? Ten percent. More?"

The real value of the quick-fix silver bullet is that it clearly gives the company the edge over the competition, because the company is reaching their own customer a little before that customer makes an independent decision to buy. The company is giving that satisfied customer a real benefit to buy a little bit earlier than when they had really wanted to, before they were even thinking of going out and kicking-the-tires and being wooed by the competition.

5. NEW CUSTOMERS FROM HEAVEN

Ground rule #5: The janitor isn't going to lead the charge for new customers.

When you travel with a pro sports team, practical jokes become part of the traveling gear.

The trainer of the Portland Trail Blazers for many years, Ron Culp, was the master of practical jokes. I swear he stayed up nights thinking of ways to pull another "gotcha." Players, coaches, executives—if you traveled with the team, you were not immune from Culp's practical jokes. You were clearly a target.

In the early 1980s, Culp got me. At least I thought so at the time. One rule of thumb in those days was that if a team had two road games in two nights, then they had to catch the first plane out of town on the day of the second game. This was a precaution against bad weather, so if one plane was canceled, another could be taken and the game would be played. This meant a lot of 7:00 A.M. departure times.

On this particular trip, our wake up call was 5:00 A.M., and we bused to the San Francisco airport, arriving about 6:00 A.M. Looking out the window, you couldn't see anything. The only thing clear was that we were fogged in. We sat and sat. About three hours later, I was being paged at the airport.

Aha, I thought, Culp is at it again. How stupid does he think I am to fall for a practical joke in front of the players, coaches, and announcers?

Those that weren't napping in their chairs—and players are the world's best at being able to sleep anyplace at any time—watched out of the corners of their eyes as I walked to pick up the page phone on the wall.

It was the executive secretary of the Blazers back in Portland. She said, "You've been traded to the Indiana Pacers."

I played along. "For what?" I asked. No executive had ever been traded before. This was starting to sound like a really lame practical joke.

"Don Buse." Buse was the Pacers starting point guard. A week before, we had lost our starting point guard, Darnell Valentine, to injury. "The Pacers want you to catch a plane from San Francisco. There is a ticket waiting for you at the United Airlines counter."

Sure. And I'm going to walk over to the United Airlines counter and ask for that ticket?

I said, "Okay," and went back to my coffee and newspaper and waited for the fog to lift. A few hours later, we were back in the office in Portland. I ran into Stu Inman, our director of player personnel, in the hallway.

He did a double take. "What are you doing here?" he said. "Didn't anybody get a hold of you? You're supposed to be going to Indianapolis."

He thrust a teletype into my face. It was from the NBA league office. Sure enough, I had been traded to the Indiana Pacers. The Blazers were to receive Don Buse. The Pacers were to receive two weeks of my time. The franchise was in a mess, and they wanted me to help get them pointed in the right direction.

Thus, on January 7, 1983, I had made a little history. I had been the first and only nonplayer in the NBA to be traded.

As I flew to Indianapolis the next day, I asked myself, "What type of practical joke is that?"

■

The problem of getting new customers isn't that companies don't want them. Every company would want new customers, I would think. The problem is that companies—even companies trying to market their way out of hell—don't want to pay the price to get new customers.

The price must be awful high, eh?

No. The dollars and cents portion of the price is, in fact, very modest. It's so modest that every company, even those firmly in hell, can afford it.

The real price is: a real commitment to get new business.

That's all? A real commitment? C'mon, there's got to be more.

Well, let's talk about real commitment and you'll see whether the price is right. By making a real commitment, I don't mean hammering your salespeople to get more new business or trying to come up with some exotic incentive for your sales staff. Real commitment to get new business means doing just three things:

1. New business has to be the top priority of the president of the company.
2. The sales staff must focus on new business.
3. Spend some money in unconventional ways to get new business.

WHAT'S MOST IMPORTANT: NEW SALES OR TALKING TO LAWYERS?

For any company that wants to jump-start itself, new business is too important to be delegated outside the president's office.

That statement might make some presidents squirm. These squirming presidents would say that they're too busy in meetings with top vice presidents of all departments in the company. They're meeting with bankers and lawyers—you know, all the people who can't bring in new business.

Let's look at how I practiced what I preached when I was president of the New Jersey Nets. First, however, we'll have to briefly look at the major revenue streams of a pro sports team.

With a pro sports team, there are three areas of revenue:

1. National TV.
2. Ticket sales.
3. Local sponsorships on radio, TV/cable, advertising signs in the arena and programs.

The individual team doesn't have any influence in increasing the revenue from national TV. Thus new business is generated from new ticket sales and new local sponsorships. Most presidents of pro teams delegate this responsibility to the VP-tickets and VP-sponsorships. My feeling is that no matter how capable the VP-tickets and the VP-sponsorships are, the president of a team can't delegate new business to them.

When I became president of the New Jersey Nets, here's how I chose *not* to delegate:

1: Sponsorship sales reported directly to me. We had five salespeople who specialized in sponsorship sales. They all reported to me. I was their department head and president.

Should I have got caught up in all those day-to-day details with sponsorship sales? You better believe it. I wanted to send the message to the staff and potential clients that sponsorships were extremely important to the New Jersey Nets. As a result, in four years we increased local sponsorship sales from $400,000 to more than $7 million.

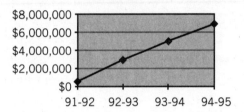

Almost all of that increase was, of course, from acquiring new sponsors. The five salespeople did all the work. They made their sales calls and, where appropriate, I tagged along. The Nets were still considered the least popular of the nine pro sports teams in the New York City area, but no other team president would make sales calls. With the New Jersey Nets, it became clear to the marketplace that sponsorships got top priority.

2: Touching ticket sales every day. At the Nets, we had over twenty full-time sales people selling ticket packages. Supervising that many salespeople on a day-to-day basis would have been too much for me. I delegated that responsibility to our VP-tickets, Jim Leahy. Since tickets are the lifeblood of pro sports teams, I did other things with the ticket salespeople so that it wouldn't even *appear* that ticket sales weren't top priority at the Nets.

To underscore the top priority that tickets had for us, I had to have a face-to-face approval meeting for the hiring of every ticket salesperson. I never turned down anybody that our VP-tickets wanted to hire. That really wasn't the issue. I just wanted to provide the mind-set for the incoming salesperson that the president of the team thought it was important enough to be involved in the selection process.

Besides meeting the new salespeople, I led our ticket sales boot camp that we held each year to "reintroduce" the sales fundamentals that we wanted our salespeople to use.

It was like baseball's spring training. Instead of practicing on the fundamentals of bunting or hitting the cutoff man, our salespeople worked on the fundamentals of getting an appointment with a new prospect or how to shift the presentation depending on the client's situation. We really put these young salespeople through the gauntlet each year. In fact, I told our VP-tickets, "If I was one of these young salespeople, I'm not sure I would go through this each year. It's brutal." He laughed and agreed. But it was essential in improving the skills of the salespeople *and* to further emphasize that the president of the company thought it was important to spend *his* week devoted to this.

Jump-Starting a Company by Just Sitting There

Additionally, I attended the twice-a-week sales meetings. I don't think any president of any pro sports team does that. If you asked some team presidents the name of their VP-tickets, these presidents would have to look it up in the team's media guide. Outside the world of sports, how many presidents of companies attend the weekly sales meetings? Presidents talk to VP-sales, not salespeople. To jump-start a company, the president needs to at least sit in on the sales meetings. Even without speaking a word, attending the sales meeting sends a huge message about the importance of sales to the company.

The following example about how a president of a pro sports team *avoided* his salespeople might seem like an extreme exaggeration, but it is fact. The story was told to me by the president of a major league baseball team. It all started when he finally found out where the ticket sales offices were.

He had noticed that his team's phone costs had gone up. It seems that this team had purchased my workbooks on ticket marketing and had taken my recommendation to add salespeople. Salespeople, of course, need phones. The president of this baseball team finally tracked down the additional phone costs. The phones had been installed in a room in the bowels of the stadium. The president walked into that room and saw a bunch of tables with a bunch of phones on them. There were young people using those phones. He confronted a young man sitting at the closest table and demanded to know who all these people were. They were, of course, salespeople selling tickets for the team.

That wasn't the case with the Nets. I, of course, knew the name of each salesperson. I also knew something about them personally and how they were doing in sales. This type of attention does take time. It takes time every day. How did I create this time? I created this time by not meeting with bankers and lawyers. I delegated that to our chief financial officer. I delegated many nonsales and nonmarketing responsibilities. After all, how could I better spend my time than by helping create new customers from heaven?

A WORD TO THE BEAN-COUNTER PRESIDENT

This roll-up-your-sleeves-and-get-involved-in-new-business attitude may make some presidents uncomfortable. This may be particularly true with the presidents who have worked their way to the top through paths other than sales/marketing. They might not have the instincts or the interest in sales. I've known presidents who are clearly more uncomfortable being with their salespeople than the salespeople are uncomfortable being with them. If that's the case, does that president then delegate the new business responsibility?

Of course not. *The president has to learn how to fit into this new business effort.* The bean-counter president might not lead this effort, but the president can be as involved as I was with the Nets. This president could attend sales meetings, make select sales calls with the salespeople, and observe the "spring training." The president would just be a little more reserved. Along the way, however, the president would be *learning* from the sales/marketing people. Because the president would be more involved in the new business process, the president would be a major force in jump-starting a company.

WHAT IF THE PRESIDENT SAYS "NO"?

Let's say that the president of the company is from the manufacturing side or the bean-counting side and won't jump in to help bring in new business. The keys to the ranch go to the top marketing person. *All* the keys.

If the president can't or won't help in marketing the company out of hell, then that president has to give full and unequivocal support to the top marketing person. If that full and unequivocal support is half-baked, the company won't be very effective with jump-start marketing.

If your company has a reluctant president, make a photocopy of this chapter and anonymously slide it under that president's door. See what happens. Maybe that president just needed a nudge.

FOCUSING ON NEW BUSINESS

In any business that is large enough to have a kitchen for its staff, have you ever noticed that nobody wants to do any housecleaning? Used cups and dishes stay in the sink. Old food gets moldy in the refrigerator. Why? You'd think that each person would sort of pick up, at least his or her own cups. Human nature doesn't seem to work that way.

The same human nature is at work with salespeople creating new business. Just like not picking up that cup in the sink and doing *something* with it, salespeople leave new business just lying around.

Try to figure it. Think what a salesperson's plight is:

- Salespeople are generally paid on a commission or bonus structure that somehow relates to sales productivity.
- Salespeople, like other employees, usually don't think they earn enough money.
- Salespeople generally don't feel that they are appreciated by top management.

The salesperson, unlike other employees, has an immediate solution to earning more money and gaining more respect. The salesperson can bring in new business. The salesperson who does that will indeed earn more money. By bringing in new business, even the stodgiest management will show some type of appreciation to that salesperson.

So why don't they do it?

Getting new business is difficult. The possibility of rejection is far greater. They have to deal with strangers. Even though the salesperson could earn more money and more recognition, it's easier to procrastinate than to go after new business. It's easy just to leave that cup in the sink.

You might answer, that's what a sales manager is for—to inspire and motivate the sales staff to go after new business. Wrong. That's the job of the president of the company, particularly for a company that needs a jump-start.

When the sales staff knows that the president of the company is truly focusing on new business, you'll see a new business culture develop. It won't be just for the money. It will also be for the recognition from the president. And, as president, you will indeed recognize the salesperson that consistently brings in new business.

SPENDING SOME CRAZY MONEY FOR NEW BUSINESS

If a company develops a new business culture, it's important to spend some money on some crazy ideas to get even more new business. I'm not recommending that a fortune be spent. That would be truly crazy. I'm talking about a pittance being spent, but a highly visible pittance on a crazy idea.

This pittance spending would serve two purposes:

1. You might actually get some new business from spending a pittance.
2. It helps underscore to your sales staff and other employees the length you will go for new business.

Let me give you a couple of examples.

When I was with the Portland Trail Blazers, I thought we were doing the best job of selling sponsorships of any team in the NBA. Even though we were in the third smallest market in the NBA, we ranked number one in radio sponsorships. We were second in television sponsorship sales. But we were also tucked away in the Pacific Northwest. While that area is a terrific place to live, it certainly isn't the center point of American capitalism. Media capitals of the United States like New York, Chicago, and Los Angeles could clearly overlook us.

So we ran an ad in an advertising trade publication with a national circulation. It cost about $3,000. In advertising trade publications, you'll see a lot of ads from different newspapers and TV stations giving demographics of their respective markets. Pretty boring stuff, but I guess that's how you do it if you're a newspaper or a TV station. Our ad was a little different.

It was a full-page ad. At a glance, you would never figure that it was an ad for a pro sports team. No action photos. Not even our logo. We wanted to reach each reader whether that reader was a sports fan or not. We decided to reach those readers with a direct response ad. Our headline said: If you could choose just one booklet, which one would it be? The sub-headline said: One could bring you $300,000, the other $13 million.

Did that catch your attention?

If you were in the advertising business, we had hoped that it would. If you read on—and how could you not—we told you some great things about the Portland Trail Blazers. You'd also find out that the $300,000 and $13 million weren't something that you could personally get. Those figures represented the sales increases that were tracked by two companies that were Blazers sponsors.

At the end of the ad, we offered your choice of two free booklets. The booklets were:

1. *Sports Marketing Evaluation.* This booklet featured different benchmarks on how to make a sports sponsorship work better for the sponsor. Perhaps by more than just a coincidence, if you used the benchmarks in this booklet, you would find that the Blazer sponsorship would be terrific for your product.
2. *Sports Marketing Case Studies.* This booklet featured actual case studies of companies that had really benefited by sports sponsorships. Each case study was, of course, a Blazer sponsor. Another coincidence?

These two booklets, by the way, were booklets that we had already had on hand as part of our proposal package to any new prospect.

With this ad, we wanted to do one thing and hopefully get a second thing accomplished as a bonus:

- Identify the Portland Trail Blazers as an innovative team that had a huge following. If you read the ad, we achieved this point. If you ordered one of the free booklets, we really hammered this point home.
- The bonus thing: Have some new business call us up.

The first thing is difficult to quantify. We think that ads helped in identifying us as a team that a company should buy a sponsorship with, even if it was way up in the Northwest.

The bonus thing was a lot easier to quantify. We didn't really think we were going to get new business from the ad. It was just a way to spend a little crazy money to tell the ad world how great we were. However, we received over $800,000 in new business! We were flabbergasted!

If we hadn't received any new business, we still would have had our fun. We would have spent our $3,000 of "mad money."

Additionally, we would have been able to use a reprint of that ad as part of a proposal for new business.

If we had received $30,000 in new business, we would have thrown a victory party. But $800,000! We didn't even know how to celebrate that type of money.

ANOTHER EXAMPLE OF CRAZY MONEY

With the New Jersey Nets, we ran a lot of direct response ads in the daily newspapers selling our different ticket packages. We tracked every phone call and order. We came up with a success grid. For every dollar that we spent in running an ad, we expected to get at least $4 back in ticket orders. If an ad achieved our ratio, we would run it again. If it didn't get our ratio, we canned it.

We would regularly run ads in New Jersey's two largest daily newspapers. That was sane and logical, since their distribution was our defined market.

What wasn't sane and logical is that we bought an ad in the national Japanese newspaper sold in the United States. Think how crazy that was. What would a Japanese person in San Francisco think when reading our ad in the *Yomiuri Times* about attending our games in *New Jersey.* Going from San Francisco to New Jersey would be some commute to see a basketball game!

There was some method to our madness. We knew that most of the Japanese companies in the United States are located in Los Angeles and the New York City area. These companies employ thousands of Americans. They also import executives—Japanese salary men. These Japanese executives are usually paid a premium to work in the United States. Also, they want to live the American experience. While basketball is not a major sport in Japan, Michael Jordan and The Shaq are major worldwide personalities. Our small ad featured Jordan, Shaq, and the young Japanese man we had hired as a local salesperson to sell those Japanese salary men.

The orders rolled in. Instead of a $4-to-$1 ratio, we were getting a $20-to-$1 ratio!

If I hadn't left the Nets, I would have spent some crazy money buying an ad in a basketball magazine printed and distributed exclusively in Japan. Again, there might have been some method to that madness. There are hundreds of thousands of Japanese who visit New York City every year. Why not go to a Nets game when visiting NYC?

On the surface, spending crazy money does seem crazy. But new business is not easy to get. Sometimes it takes some crazy money to spend on some crazy ideas to see if they work.

GETTING NEW BUSINESS AIN'T EASY

Many companies wait for a hot new product that will hand deliver new business to their doors. Some companies even wait their way out of existence. While I'm a huge believer in innovation (see chapter 7), I also believe that a company can't wait for innovation to bail it out.

What bails out a company is a total and real commitment to getting new business. And the commitment starts at the top.

A Simple Test You Can Take

(Circle the answer.) **Which of the three things a company should do to make a real commitment to new business does your company not do?**

1. New business is the top priority of the president of our company.

Yes   No

2. The sales staff clearly focuses on new business.

Yes   No

3. We spend some money in unconventional ways to get new business.

Yes   No

(Fill in the blanks.) **Identify three areas where you could spend some crazy money to get some new business.**

A. _____

B. _____

C. _____

Answers

1: I've never seen a company jump-start itself from the bottom up. The president of the company—or at least those vice presidents near the top—need to take the jump-start initiative. If you're not the president or one of the top VPs, there is still some hope. You'll have to form your own terrorist group for jump-starting. It's relatively easy to form a terrorist group for jump-starting. Read chapter 8 for the blueprint.

2: During a speech, I recommended that companies spend some crazy money on getting some new ideas. During the Q & A part of the speech, one guy stood up and said, "We really run a tight ship. We would never allow crazy money to be spent."

"For new business?" I asked.

"For no purpose would we," he said, jutting out his jaw.

I yelled out to him, "Watch out! Duck!" Some people around did duck their heads. He didn't flinch.

"I think companies should run a tight ship," I said. "But without spending some crazy money on new business—and I don't mean a significant amount of money—you're not pushing yourself enough, you're not taking enough chances to get new business. Your whole company could come tumbling down on you. You could slide into hell and wouldn't even know you slid until you started to feel the heat. Spend some crazy money for new business. The bankruptcy judge never compliments a company because they ran a tight ship."

6. PAYING BONUSES FOR MISTAKES

Ground rule #6: Create big change with little experiments.

"Going to the dark side."

If you remember, that was the concern that Luke Skywalker would join Darth Vader. The first time I heard that phrase, however, was not in the movie *Star Wars*. It was from my father.

My father was a sports writer for the *Detroit News* for over thirty years. He had covered the Detroit Lions during their halcyon days when Bobby Layne was the quarterback. He also covered the Detroit Tigers when they won a pennant. That was 1968, and Denny McLain won thirty-one games.

During that time, I had been in normal nonsports businesses working my way up the ladder. In 1977, I took a curve in my career path and went to work for the Buffalo Braves, a team in the NBA.

After the Braves and I had agreed, I called up my dad. I told him that I was the new VP of marketing for the Buffalo Braves. There was a pause on the phone.

"You mean you've gone to the dark side," he said. Teams and sportswriters were like the snake and the mongoose.

Before I could answer, he said, "But God has strange ways." He was still a sportswriter then, and maybe he thought I could be a good inside source. You know, if you're a newspaper writer, it would be handy to have a Deep Throat in the family.

It seemed like my dad was right, although not in the way he thought. Working for the Braves seemed like I was on the dark side. While I would have to be considered a failure with the Braves—the team moved after ten months—it was in Buffalo that I first started to learn the principles of jump-start marketing.

That learning started on the first day. In recruiting me, the Braves had lied. They had said they had 5,000 season ticket holders. The fact was that when I got there in August, they had less than fifty. It seems that the previous owner had threatened to move the team (how times don't change) unless 5,000 season tickets were sold. The corporations in Buffalo really got behind the drive, and the ticket target was reached. The day after that, the owner sold the leading scorer in the league, Bob McAdoo, to the Knicks. Then he sold two other starters. In effect, he cashed in on the 5,000 season tickets and then liquidated the club and sold it to John Y. Brown.

Obviously and deservedly so, the fans were furious over the past year. There were fifty hardy souls who did renew. For us to increase ticket sales above fifty, we had to sell people that had never been to a Braves game before. Which we did. We sold about 3,000 season tickets in an impossible situation using the embryonic principles of jump-start marketing.

However, less than a year later, the Braves fulfilled their destiny. They became the San Diego Clippers, eventually becoming the Los Angeles Clippers. The Clippers have never done well in the NBA. I wonder if this is the Curse of Bob McAdoo?

Just recently I heard that "dark side" phrase again.

The chief of staff of a state's governor called me. They were in the midst of trying to save their team from moving to a more lucrative pasture. (See how these sports stories keep repeating themselves?)

The state had offered to build a stadium, but the team was giving them estimates on how much revenue could be generated with the sale of the title sponsorship of the stadium, advertising, suites, preferred seating, etc. The state wanted to hire me as their expert in evaluating whether the team's figures were too low or too high.

"Will you have any problems with other teams?" the chief of staff asked.

"No," I said. "Why do you ask?"

"Well, it might be considered that you're going to the dark side . . ."

I laughed.

It seems that each situation can have a "dark side" or "another side." I think over the years that I have experienced all the sides. The side that I know and appreciate is the side that is innovative in marketing and looks to jump-start on a regular basis. That side is definitely not the dark side, and it's the side to be on.

■

Before I resigned from the Nets, I had been fiddling around with a concept about paying people bonuses for making mistakes. I'm not talking about simple mistakes like a typing error or leaving the office coffee machine on over the weekend. I'm talking about *bigger* mistakes.

You may think that with this type of concept it was good that I resigned before I could implement such a crazy idea and do some real damage. Firing wouldn't be the mode of action for the owners. The guillotine would be their first choice. *Then* fire the bastard!

The mistakes I would have been paying for were the same mistakes that I had been looking for and encouraging for years. These were mistakes made by trying to innovate.

I think I came up with a pretty good formula, and I'll explain it later in this chapter. First, I want to talk about the role that innovation has in keeping jump-start marketing jumping. In fact, I feel that innovation is so important, I devote this chapter and the next two chapters to it.

WHY WOULD I RESORT TO SUCH A CRAZY IDEA AS TO PAY PEOPLE TO MAKE MISTAKES?

By incorporating just a few of the jump-start suggestions in this book, you will bring about a change in your organization. That's not enough. To keep the growth that jump-starting will initiate, your organization or department has to *live* change.

As we all know, people don't like to change. Sure it's a cliché, but it's true. People may talk about how a company should change some things when they're standing around the water cooler or having a drink with office friends after work. Yes, they will informally *talk* change, but few want to *live* change. I'm talking about walk in every morning and face change eyeball-to-eyeball all day long.

This type of change really isn't as scary as it might sound. The changes that I have in mind aren't major changes, but slight changes, slight improvements in everything a company does. The jump-start principles are a wonderful catalyst to initiate change without frightening everybody who works there. But what keeps jump-start marketing going?

In jump-starting a company, you're starting the movement of growth, but that growth will stop dead in its tracks if the jump-start principles are shelved once growth is under way.

You need "little innovations," which, of course, are little changes, to keep the jump-start momentum. That momentum will automatically lead to big, breakthrough innovations.

DISGUISING CHANGE

If you say that "your people will have to *live* change," you most likely will have effectively put the fear of God into everyone. When they've got that type of fear, they stop thinking, they stop any effort at being innovative. So to develop a culture where you are living change, you have to do it in non-threatening edible bites that don't look like change.

There's a good reason for disguising change into edible bites. Over a period of time, many employees have developed scar tissue that protects them from even *thinking* change. This scar tissue was formed, layer by layer, when these employees saw fingers of blame regularly pointed at people making mistakes of some sort. In some cases, the finger might have been pointed at them.

Even if a company is headed to hell, the layer upon layer of scar tissue that was acquired prevents employees from being innovative, except perhaps on their résumés that they were running through the copy machine at night.

What I have found is that while employees don't like change, they don't mind "little experiments." Experiments are, after all, experimental, or temporary. It's not real change. It's just experimentation.

At the Nets, we had so many "little experiments" going on that we were changing daily, improving daily. Nobody saw any sweeping broad-brush changes, because there weren't any. Without those sweeping changes, there wasn't any reason to be threatened. But was there change! In fact, when it came to experimenting, employees showed more enthusiasm, more camaraderie, for these experiments than they did for their regular responsibilities. And they started to *think*. Every day. They started to innovate. Every day.

JUMP-STARTING "LITTLE EXPERIMENTS"

These little experiments help push employees into living change. One word of caution, however. Even when they are living change, don't expect employees to come up with breakthrough ideas.

Employees prefer to suggest. Don't think that's not enough. It is. Once they are living change, those suggestions can lead to breakthrough thinking.

One of the ways that I tried to increase the number of suggestions from the Nets staff was at a think-tank session. I held similar-type sessions for each of the eleven years that I worked for the Portland Trail Blazers. The first one had just four people attending. That was our marketing department. It never ceased to amaze me how simple suggestions turned into some terrific solutions to some perplexing problems. The suggestions catapulted us to growth. In fact, the last think-tank session that I attended with the Blazers had fifty people in attendance.

For two weeks before these sessions, each employee had some homework to do. Each person was required to come up with five ideas a day on how to improve what we were doing for a living. No pressure to come up with breakthrough ideas here. They were told not to be the judge and jury of these ideas, but to just jot down these ideas, however ridiculous they may seem at the time. Their ridiculous ideas would be safe from public scrutiny—the ideas were never photocopied and distributed. The ideas were their personal idea bank.

If each employee came up with five ideas a day from Monday through Friday and didn't even think on the weekends, each would come to the think-tank sessions armed with fifty ideas on how we could improve.

At each think-tank session, I would choose a topic—like how do we renew 95 percent of our season ticket holders—and these topics acted as a funnel to pour ideas into. No matter what the topic was, at least a few suggestions from each person's bank of fifty ideas would surface.

I'll give you an example.

Armed with the thought process that brought about fifty ideas, one of our sponsorship sales people asked during a coffee break at the think tank, "Why do the press get to sit behind the team benches?"

The three or four of us sitting there looked at each other like idiots. During these frozen moments, our questioner said, "In every other arena, they have fans sitting behind the benches. Why can't we put our sponsors there instead of the press?"

At the time, nobody said that this was a breakthrough idea that would lead to a $1 million profit center that didn't exist before that question was asked.

The answer to his question is a little silly. The media sat right behind the team benches because they always had.

The Nets ticket demand had never been so great to where they felt that they could actually *sell* those seats. Once it was established for the media, it was set in stone. Well, as others started to come back into the room, we had brought out the jackhammer.

The first part of the discussion led to putting seats behind the benches for the fans. Somebody did a quick tally of what those seats would be worth.

Then somebody said, "Signage."

Instead of putting sponsors in behind the bench, this staff member suggested that we put in the same type of advertising signs that were at the scorer's table. Thirty feet of signage behind each bench. When you sell this type of signage, the real value comes from its high visibility on TV. When the TV camera was focused on either basket, which was most of the time, the camera couldn't frame a shot without our advertising signs in the upper third of the picture. This is valuable stuff.

We conceptualized this signage package, pulled and pinched and squashed it, and then smoothed it out and put a price tag on it to see how it would feel. It felt pretty good. Six months later, we had sold that signage package, and it brought in $1 million directly to the bottom line. It was like walking down the street and finding a million dollars just sitting there, in small unmarked bills.

NO STANDING OVATIONS

When you look at it, nobody ever came up with a breakthrough idea, explained it to the group, and everybody stood up and cheered. Each breakthrough idea started with a suggestion for improving something we were doing. It was so simple. It was nonthreatening. It was just a *suggestion*. Or a "stupid" question. A suggestion that took a life of its own and became a profit center.

EVEN GETTING SUGGESTIONS ISN'T EASY AT FIRST

Now suppose we would have tied a bonus to these suggestions? Surely that would have increased the amount of suggestions. But what about paying a bonus only for making a suggestion that eventually failed? Wouldn't that remove a lot of the scar tissue? Wouldn't it make it more socially accept-able to make suggestions?

Why give a bonus for failure? Why not only for suggestions that lead to success? There are two good reasons for giving a bonus for a failure.

1: They're paid for success anyway. The people who attended these think-tank sessions were all sales/marketing people. Each was on some type of a bonus program that increased their income when we increased revenue. If a suggestion was made that was converted into a revenue-producing product, they all benefited in their normal compensation. For instance, if an experiment was tried, became successful, expanded, and became part of our everyday work life, it was part of their com-pensation. That's what happened with our signage behind the teams' benches. There was over $50,000 paid in bonuses for that project.

2: Better suggestions, better ideas, better chances. When the curse is removed from failure, my feeling is that people produce better suggestions. Better suggestions lead to better product ideas or improvements. Better product ideas lead to a better chance of success. A better chance of success leads to more revenue. More revenue generally leads to more profit.

Paying for making mistakes is really a "security blanket" to encourage more suggestions. By no means do I mean that you approve every suggestion. But the people involved in the ones that are approved, and eventually fail, should receive a bonus.

By paying for failure, you'll find that fewer ideas will fail. This is mainly because the unbridled suggestions will lead to ideas that are of the breakthrough variety. A naysayer would comment, "If people are paid for failures, they will target those projects and cause them to fail."

That thinking goes against human nature. People would much prefer to see their idea succeed. And the cash bonus for failure isn't a lot of money. Maybe $500. If it were $100,000, then that person might actively submarine the idea. But nobody would submarine their own idea for only $500.

So, again, why spend money for failure? Why spend the $500? The bonus would underscore the company's focus on thinking process for new ideas, new improvements. After all, you're even willing to pay for failure.

Something simple like paying $500 for an idea that flopped sends a very powerful message that keeps jump-start marketing flourishing. Just the thought of paying for failure would go a long way in establishing the corporate culture of innovate, innovate, innovate, and when you're tired, innovate some more.

A Simple Test You Can Take

(Fill in the blanks.) **While employees don't like _____, they don't mind "little _____."**

(Fill in the blanks.) **Paying for mistakes is a crazy idea. However, you'd like to try it. There is a problem. The way your company is structured, you'd never be able to give cash as a bonus. There are other things, however, that you could give. List those other things:**

A. _____

B. _____

C. _____

Answers

1: While employees don't like *change*, they don't mind "little *experiments*."

2: Getting people to think and innovate is very difficult. Paying for mistakes is just one way to underscore the importance of being innovative. However, getting the boss to approve such a crazy idea may be even more difficult than getting people to think and innovate. What could take the place of cash for rewarding failure?

It could be bonus days off. This would be pretty easy to do. Just tell the person to take off the day or week. You can probably cover that. While easy, it's not as good as cash, nor is it nearly as dramatic in sending a message about innovation. So what else do you have other than being able to give a few days off? Free travel? Free food?

C'mon, there's got to be something! Come up with something neat. Whatever you find, you most likely won't have to use it. Paying for failure is mainly a prop to emphasize your era of innovation. If, by chance, you finally do have to pay for failure, you will have had so many grand-slam home runs brought to you by innovation you could fly the person around the world and not one eyebrow would be lifted.

7. INNOVATE, INNOVATE, INNOVATE, AND WHEN YOU'RE TIRED, INNOVATE SOME MORE

Ground rule #7: Don't wait for a new product to bail you out—use innovative marketing now.

One of the problems that we faced in marketing the Nets was that the team lacked identity in the state of New Jersey. That seems to happen to teams that adopt a state name instead of a city name.

Only a few teams are named after their state. Does it seem like someone was embarrassed about something? Should Indianapolis be proud that the team named itself the Indiana Pacers? Should Oakland be proud that their team is named the Golden State Warriors? How about Anaheim? Instead of the Anaheim Angels, the city got the California Angels.

What if other teams named themselves after the state? Would the Chicago Cubs sound as good as the Illinois Cubs? Would the Boston Red Sox sound as good as the Massachusetts Red Sox? Of course not.

The Nets home city is East Rutherford. East Rutherford, New Jersey, is where the Meadowlands Complex is located. It's a huge swamp on which the state built Giants Stadium, Meadowlands Racetrack, and Meadowlands Arena, where the Nets and Devils play.

So, East Rutherford Nets? East Rutherford Nets sounds awful. We were talking about this one day before a staff meeting. Then Joe Macdonell, our box office VP, said, "Why not change the name of East Rutherford?"

We stopped and stared at Joe. He wasn't kidding.

"It's been done before," Joe said. "About ten years ago, there used to be a West Patterson. These people didn't want to be associated with the slums of Patterson, so they changed the name of their town to Rolling Brook."

"What's the population of East Rutherford?" I asked.

"Maybe ten thousand," Joe said.

We all saw what was coming. It was like somebody had turned on a bright light in a dark room: title sponsorship of a pro team.

We dispatched our chief financial officer, Ray Schaetzle, over to East Rutherford's city hall to do a little undercover work. He found out that the city could change it's name only by a popular vote. That meant that we'd have to get about five hundred signatures to get a "change the name" on a voter referendum.

Ray dug a little further. The tax base of East Rutherford was only about $10 million. "If people got a thirty percent reduction in taxes," Ray said, "they'd change their city name."

We thought of companies that would like to have this little town named after them. Nike was the first corporation that we thought of. They were maverick enough to see the bigger, and outrageous, picture: the Nike Nets.

In the newspapers around the world, it would be the Nike Nets. On ESPN Sports Center, it would be the Nike Nets. When "Monday Night Football" on ABC broadcast a game from Giants Stadium, Al Michaels would be saying, "From Nike, New Jersey, it will be the New York Giants against . . . "

The NBA forbids corporate names or logos on team uniforms. They don't forbid, of course, the city name on team uniforms. Like *Chicago* Bulls. Like *Detroit* Tigers.

Even if Nike bought the team, they couldn't put their name on the uniform. Only the originating city and the nickname. Nike Nets. Nike wouldn't have to buy a multimillion-dollar licensing deal from the NBA to get worldwide exposure.

The Nets were the only pro team in the United States that could do this. What would it cost to get Los Angeles to change their name? Thirty percent of its tax base would be in the billions of dollars.

When we got together again, I wrote down $5 million on the blackboard. The East Rutherford tax coffers would get $3 million, the team would get $2 million.

While this would take a vote from the East Rutherford residents, we thought money could talk. It would also distinguish East Rutherford. The name Nike would be a lot more fun than East Rutherford. Land values might even go up.

Changing the name of the city was an outrageous idea. It wouldn't be easy. Think of the impossible steps. First, sell Nike on the prospect of the "title sponsorship" of a city. Nike would have to commit on a "get-the-vote-and-we'll-do-it" basis. Second, get the referendum. Third, get the popular vote. The task would be far too daunting. But would it have been fun!

It was even fun talking about it. I knew then that the staff was buying into innovation. They were starting to think crazy, outrageous ideas. This type of thinking was absolutely necessary for us to catapult the Nets beyond jump-start marketing.

Hmm . . . Nike Nets.

■

A golfing friend of mine asked me if I wanted to buy a partnership in the used golf cart that he was going to buy. The cart cost only $500. I usually like to walk while playing golf, but for $250 I thought it was a cheap enough investment for the days when my feet were sore.

A week later, I was at the club and my friend unveiled our new purchase. It looked pretty good. It even had a roof and side curtains for when it rained.

The cart ran on gas. "Let me show you how to put gas in it," my friend said. He went to the front of the cart and pulled back a lever. He then lifted the entire cab of the cart backward, pivoting it on a hinge attached to the chassis. "C'mon and help me," he said, struggling with it.

I grabbed on to one side. "I thought you were going to put gas in it," I said. "I don't need to see anything else."

"That's what we're going to do. Gas it up."

With the cab of the cart perpendicular to the ground, my friend pointed to the engine. It looked like a lawn mower engine. It even had a gas cap.

"That's where you put the gas," he said, pulling the gas cap off.

Incredible!

The maker of the cart was Harley Davidson. The same Harley Davidson that makes biker hogs. I guess they didn't have the experience of building an engine that didn't have a gas cap extended away from the tank by a pipe or tube.

Once we gassed up, we played a round of golf. At the end of the day, we stunk. I'm not referring to our games. We smelled like we had been sitting all day behind a smoke-belching bus. The reason was that Harley Davidson had not put an exhaust pipe on the cart. The exhaust pipe was not lost or stolen, the engineers at Harley Davidson had never included one! There wasn't even a place for one. The exhaust would just flow out of the engine and seep up to where we sat in the cab. On a windy day, though, it wasn't so bad.

I've always been amazed by that golf cart. How in the world did the engineers ever design that golf cart? At some time, did one of them say, "Hey, we forgot to put in a tube to pour in the gas. And, *wow*, we forgot to put in an exhaust pipe!" Was the answer, "Forget it. We'll just have these poor slobs lift the front of the cab all the way back. Here, hand me that hinge. I'll hook it on the back. And forget the exhaust. Nobody will ever notice."

That Harley Davidson golf cart was a lousy product. But somebody had to market it. While that person probably couldn't make any dramatic, immediate improvements, that person could have at least *started* to get the process going that would have added a tube for the gas and an exhaust pipe.

Let's suppose for the moment that somehow that marketing person convinced the engineers to add a tube for gas and an exhaust pipe. And let's say that it took them only six months to improve the product. Mission accomplished, right?

Wrong.

Innovation is a process that no company can afford to stop, even after a tube to the gas tank and an exhaust pipe have been added.

INNOVATION AS A WAY OF LIFE

In chapter 6, I wrote about paying bonuses for mistakes as a prop to underscore the degree you are willing to go to for innovation. In almost any industry, the best role model for innovation is the high-tech business. They *can't* sit back and stop innovating. If they did, in three to six months they would be woefully behind. With these high-tech companies, innovation is not optional.

My feeling is that any company needs to innovate all the time just to survive. I'm not referring to major breakthrough products here. I'm talking about:

1: Little innovations. These innovations can improve existing products—like adding an exhaust pipe. Remember, you're looking for attributes to market the product or company that you have. A small, inexpensive innovation could give you another attribute—or even just a second attribute—to market.

Sure, you would like the company to add an exhaust pipe or a tube for gas, but most marketing people don't have the clout to drive product improvements. Your job is to market the product that you are given. The little innovations I'm going to refer to in this chapter are just that: little marketing innovations.

Yes, life would be much more simpler and fun if all of our products were perfect products with no warts and pimples. But I haven't known that type of a world. If one day I do, maybe there won't be a place for me in that perfect world. After all, the product people would say that the product is so perfect it markets itself.

2: New product innovations. If you are in the automobile business, we're talking about a huge investment—in the range of billions of dollars. However, most people are now employed in service businesses. In these businesses, you can usually come up with new products at a modicum of expense. New products in service industries usually start by employee suggestions if the company has set up a culture of innovation.

When I arrived at the Nets, innovation was a four-letter word. This, by the way, was not that unusual in pro sports teams. Nor is it at all unusual for most companies.

For some odd reason, and I don't know that reason, many pro sports teams would routinely hide from new marketing ideas behind these two phrases:

1. "That won't work in my market."
2. "My market is different."

I've known many nonsports companies that use the same two lines. It's bull. As we know, good marketing principles work in any market. Sure, they might have to be fine-tuned a little, but good marketing works anywhere.

CHANGING THE CULTURE

As you know by now, I feel that innovation should be a daily thing. But one of the best ways to jump-start innovation is with the think-tank sessions away from the office. We did just that with the New Jersey Nets.

We took most of our salespeople to Atlantic City for a three-day think tank. At the think tank, we made some assumptions and challenges. I did set up some ground rules for innovation, but these ground rules were set up mainly to keep us on track. The ground rules were:

1: Our product wasn't going to bail us out. The easiest way for us to jump-start our company was to improve our product, which was the team. That's the quickest way for any company. In our case, we would just add Michael Jordan and The Shaq, and we're overnight marketing geniuses. Unfortunately, like most companies, we can't just push a button and come out with a super product.

Our meeting was for marketing people. Our collective vote in improving our product—or dramatically changing the makeup of the team—was the same as yours. No vote. So this meeting was *not* how to improve our product on the floor. Whatever time we spent think-tanking on how to improve the team would have been wasted time. That's the reason for this ground rule: Our product wasn't going to bail us out. This was a meeting about how to better market the product that was given to us. We can't change the warts and pimples, but we don't have to highlight them in our marketing.

This isn't all that unusual. Most marketers can't expect their product to undergo a dramatic improvement that will have the product selling itself. The Nets situation would be like the situation with the Harley Davidson golf carts—market the product that you are given, however awful it may be.

2: Define a marketing area where we could have a chance to succeed. Remember, our product limited us in our marketing. Thus, we wanted to concentrate in areas where we had the best chance of succeeding.

We felt that we had a chance to sell tickets to our biggest games—those against the Orlando Magic, Chicago Bulls and New York Knicks. We would spend all of our think-tank energies in creating strategies where we had a chance for success—our biggest games—and spend no time working on areas where we had little chance for success—the other games on our schedule.

3: Create strategies in the defined areas where there was a chance for success. We felt that by packaging those big games together, we would be able to get more sellouts.

Sellouts by themselves are one of the best marketing tools for a pro sports team. If fans know that there are plenty of seats for every game, they will procrastinate their purchases and eventually might not buy at all. If the fans realize that the best games will sell out, they will purchase ticket packages months in advance.

Our seven-game ticket packages were vital to selling out the arena. These sellouts gave us the momentum and confidence to create even more sellouts. The following is our sellout record and where we wanted to go:

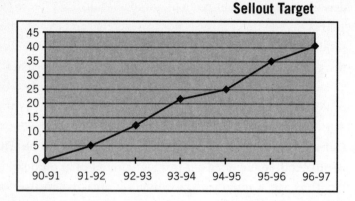

Sellout Target

4: Create new applications for our product. In this case, our product was tickets.

You might think that a ticket to a basketball game is a ticket to a basketball game. That thinking is too limited. That type of thinking would never have allowed Arm & Hammer Baking Soda to be marketed as a deodorant for a refrigerator.

We specifically wanted to create a new application for our tickets to megacorporations. We were doing a decent job of selling season tickets to corporations. However, most of these corporate buyers were the smaller and medium-size corporations. The reason for this was that our salespeople could get an appointment with the president of a company that size. When it came to the bigger corporations, and in northern New Jersey there were many Fortune 500 companies, it was much tougher to make an appointment with the president. When we did get an appointment, our sales pitch didn't really fit these megacorporations, with their thousands of employees, worldwide sales, and an army of vice presidents. Clearly, we needed a "bigger product" than just four season tickets.

Bigger product? This is where we had to innovate. We needed to sell these megacorporations much more than four season tickets. We needed to have these megacorporations help us sell out more games.

TOM PETERS, HARVEY MACKAY, LOU HOLTZ, AND DERRICK COLEMAN?

Using the four ground rules, we came up with a new product idea that was targeted to these megacorporations. The new product had to be more than just an appeal to support the local pro team with more season tickets. To help us, we brought in Tom Peters, Harvey Mackay, and Lou Holtz.

This new ticket product was, in essence, a three-game season ticket. At each of these three games, we would have a pregame motivational speaker. The celebrity speaker would begin at 5:30 P.M. and talk for a little less than an hour. The audience would then have about an hour to get something to eat and drink before tip-off. There was no premium charged to hear the speakers before the game.

These speakers weren't cheap, of course. Let's look at the math. The average cost for the speakers was about $40,000 each. Our seats downstairs cost $54.50 each. So all we had to do was sell 733 tickets to each of these three games to break even. But breaking even wasn't our goal. We wanted to significantly increase our gate for these games and achieve three more sellouts in the process. It's too bad that everything in life isn't this easy!

With one of our young salespeople, I would go out to see the presidents of these megacorporations. After hearing any of the presidents of those megacorporations rant about how lousy the Nets were, I would say, "So? Let me tell you how we can help you." I would then describe the three-game season ticket package.

A typical response was, "How many of these packages can we buy?" This was a stunner. At the Nets, we had never heard that question before!

My response was, "How many do you want to buy?"

"Seven hundred and fifty?"

If you do the math—each package cost $163.50—the total for that sale was $122,625!

The sale didn't end there. As almost an afterthought, I would say, "By the way, you don't have season tickets to the Nets. You should have eight. That would cost only $16,000."

"Yeah, okay." End of sale.

We scoured northern New Jersey for big corporations. One company had over 2,000 employees, and I had never even heard of them. They were an oil refinery in Elizabeth, New Jersey. They bought $70,000 worth of tickets.

In the first week, we had paid for the three guest speakers. In subsequent weeks, we were paving the way to three more sellouts. These sellouts were juicy ones, because the games were against the NBA's worst attractions—the expansion teams and the Minnesota Timberwolves. We were finally going to sell out a Timberwolves-Nets game!

Speakers and Basketball

	Before Speakers	Projected with Speakers
Ticket sales per game	$300,000	$600,000
Ticket sales for three games	$900,000	$1,800,000
Sellout potential	Are you kidding?	Yes

Let's take a quick look at how innovation worked with our product:

- **The product was the same.** We didn't add Michael Jordan or The Shaq to the team. It was the same cast of characters that our fans had grown to hate.

- **The retail area was the same.** Meadowlands Arena hadn't changed. It was still the same 20,000 seats.

- **The packaging was different.** What was different was that we dramatically enhanced our packaging. We added three exciting speakers to make the games much bigger than they were. By packaging, we were selling a "three-game season ticket." When big corporations bought 750 packages, they were buying 2,250 tickets. This was the equivalent to almost fifty-five forty-one-game season tickets!

  These three highly recognizable motivational speakers helped blur the fact that we didn't have a very good product. It also helped blur the fact that our basketball opponents weren't very good attractions either.

  This worked for us at the time because we were selling out over half of our schedule with our other ticket packages featuring the best opponents with marquee players. If we weren't selling out the arena as often, I'm not sure that the speakers would have had as big of an impact for these awful games.

Everything was the same, except we added an innovative three-game season ticket. Besides the increase in sales that this three-game season ticket brought us, for the first time we were developing relationships with the area's largest corporations.

A month later, I held a think-tank session with our sponsorship people. We used the same ground rules:

1. Our product wasn't going to bail us out.
2. Define a marketing area where we could have a chance to succeed.
3. Create strategies in the defined areas where there was a chance for success.
4. Create new applications for our products.

Because our people had forced themselves to go through the thinking process of arming themselves with fifty ideas *and* we had certain ground rules, a simple question led to a breakthrough idea. That was the signage behind the teams benches that brought over $1 million in profit the next season.

WHAT TO DO WHEN THE BOSS DOESN'T WANT INNOVATION

If you've been in business, you've been the victim of a boss who doesn't want innovation. It's unavoidable. Quitting a job to try to find a boss that will encourage innovation is a wasted exercise.

Innovation can start with whoever has this book in their hands. That means you. However, being the lone innovator in your department can be hazardous to your health and your career. You can take a step that will improve your safety and your clout. Form a terrorist group.

Forming a terrorist group for innovation isn't really that difficult to do—if you have a game plan. The next two chapters are simple and effective game plans to form your own terrorist group for innovation.

Once you have a terrorist group for innovation, you can

host your own think-tank sessions. These think-tank sessions don't have to be held on company time and they don't have to be held at a resort. They could be held in somebody's basement on a weekend. The important thing is to innovate *someplace* and have the mechanism in place to sell that innovation to a boss that doesn't want to innovate.

You think that's too big of a challenge?

Not at all. Convincing a boss who doesn't want to innovate is the *easy* part. In fact, what you do to the boss who doesn't want to innovate is downright unfair, as you'll see in chapter 8. What's needed is innovation. So innovate, innovate, innovate, and when you're tired, innovate some more.

A Simple Test You Can Take

(Fill in the blanks.) **In what two areas can marketing people be innovative in a think-tank session?**

A. _____

B. _____

(Fill in the blanks.) **What are the four ground rules for a think-tank session among marketing people?**

A. _____

B. _____

C. _____

D. _____

Answers

1. A. *Little marketing innovations.* As much as I would like you to have a breakthrough product that jump-starts your com-

pany, or even a marketing breakthrough, look for little innovations. Look for another attribute that you can use in marketing your product or company.

B. *Product innovations (if you are a service company).* New products for service companies usually don't cost billions or even millions or even thousands of dollars. Here's where your marketing people can be innovative in creating a product like we did with the signage behind the team benches.

2. These four ground rules should work to help your people focus on suggestions where you can do something.
   A. Our product wasn't going to bail us out.
   B. Define a marketing area where we could have a chance to succeed.
   C. Create strategies in the defined areas where there was a chance for success.
   D. Create new applications for your product.

8. CREATING YOUR OWN TERRORIST GROUP FOR INNOVATION

Ground rule #8: To get your ideas approved by the boss, prepare as if you were defending yourself in front of the Supreme Court.

This little episode might have seen its first spark when we were talking about the Nike Nets. Like a lot of innovation, it started with just a conversation.

First, let me give you a little background.

At the Nets, we thought that changing the name of East Rutherford was too daunting. Instead, we started to take an easier path and thought about changing our logo. For years, Nets merchandise had ranked last in sales for teams in the NBA. A major part of the reason was that the team was consistently lousy. But there was more. The Charlotte Hornets were an expansion team in 1990, and they were lousy for several years. And yet the Hornets ranked in the top five in NBA merchandise sales.

It wasn't just people in Charlotte buying the stuff. Charlotte was doing well in worldwide sales in places like Tokyo, Brussels, and Tijuana. The reason for their success was the style of their merchandise. Designer Alexander Julian had designed their uniforms using teal as the main color. Additionally, he added pinstripes to the uniform.

Teal was a hot color for team merchandise that fans bought. The Nets colors were old and boring—red, white, and blue.

We didn't want to increase our merchandise sales because we were hoping for some financial windfall. There wouldn't be such a windfall, because all NBA teams share equally in licensed merchandise sales. For instance, when the Chicago Bulls won three straight championships and everyone was buying Bulls T-shirts, sweatshirts, and jackets, the Nets received the same amount of money from those sales as the Chicago Bulls. We wanted more fans to wear our merchandise to raise the positive awareness levels of the Nets.

The NBA has a creative department. We talked to them. They worked on the project for awhile. At a meeting, they told us that there really wasn't any hope. Sure, we could change colors, but our logo was still a net. That would be like the New York Giants being named the New York Goalposts. Or the New York Yankees being named the New York Second Bases.

What was working in today's world were characters of some sort that could be animated. The Hornet's logo was a hornet. You know, the type of bug that can sting you. Expansion teams were named after characters that could be animated, like the Raptors of Toronto or the Grizzlies of Vancouver.

One morning, I was talking to Jim Lampariello, the Nets executive VP. I was looking out my window at a swamp. You see, the Nets are located in what the politicians refer to as a meadowland. In reality, it is a swamp.

Many sports teams have nicknames that are indigenous to their areas: Portland Trail Blazers (you know, the Oregon Trail), Seattle Supersonics (Boeing is up there), San Antonio Spurs, Miami Heat, Boston Celtics (all those Irish in Boston), etc.

I said to Jim, "I keep on coming back to the word 'swamp' as part of a new nickname. But then I always come up with 'rat,' and I'm not sure that's terrific to have."

"Dragons," Jim said.

"Huh?"

"Dragons. Swamp Dragons. Dragons are mythical, they can come from anywhere, even a swamp. Kids love dragons. Dragons are loved throughout the world. . . ."

We jumped in a car and drove to NBA Creative, which was located just three miles down the road. They loved it. They started working on it before we had left the building. Within two days, we had the design. It was a ferocious-looking dragon. In swamp teal. People in the NBA office thought that we would be ranked in the top three in merchandise sales *in the world.* Add a moral victory when fans going to Knicks games in New York had their kids wearing New Jersey Swamp Dragons merchandise to the game.

We had a long process to get it approved. We formed a terrorist group for innovation. We followed the steps to take that are explained in this chapter. We presented the idea to the Nets owners. Surprisingly, they were enthusiastic.

We presented the idea to David Stern, the commissioner of the NBA. He turned it over to the executive committee, a group of powerful owners. After making the presentation, they said they would support a motion to change the Nets name to Swamp Dragons.

There were to be twenty-nine votes on the issue, each one representing an NBA team. We needed to get a majority vote, or fifteen votes, to change the name.

We worked the teams like politicians work the electoral votes. The vote came in at 28–1 in favor of changing the name from New Jersey Nets to New Jersey Swamp Dragons.

Unfortunately, the one dissenting vote was the New Jersey Nets. At the last minute, one of the seven Nets owners got cold feet, and the Nets voted no.

■

In my four and a half years with the New Jersey Nets, there's only one idea that wasn't approved by my Supreme Court—the seven New Jersey Nets owners. That one exception was changing the name from Nets to Swamp Dragons.

It wasn't a fluke that we got that many approvals, and it wasn't easy. Remember, there were seven owners of the Nets. Each one was very successful, and each one had distinct opinions about how things should be done. What gave us our seemingly miraculous high approval rate was that we regularly formed terrorist groups for innovation.

CREATING A TERRORIST GROUP CULTURE

If you're the president of a company, terrific. Start building a new culture of innovation to jump-start your company. If you're less than a president, terrific. Start building a new culture to jump-start the company that you work for. To do this, however, you may need some help. You may need a terrorist group for innovation.

Here are a few semi-simple steps to start innovation anywhere:

1: **Recruit a soul mate:** When I started as VP-marketing with the Portland Trail Blazers in 1979, it was the Ice Age of sports business. Fans were left up to their own motivations to buy tickets. If they wanted to go to a game, they bought a ticket. If they didn't want to go to a game, they didn't buy a ticket.

This was at the beginning of an era of multimillion-dollar player contracts, which would change the front offices of sports teams throughout the country. In this new era, no longer could a team just wait for fans to buy tickets or wait for a company to buy a sponsorship. Teams had to start using what was then considered a four-letter word: marketing. In this new era, it became marketing for survival.

In 1979, there were only eleven employees in the Blazers front office. That included two in accounting, one receptionist, one player personnel guy, one president, one hanger-on, a promotions director, three in the box office, and me. The other ten of them had fully subscribed to absolutely no change in anything except for the playing roster. The president used to regularly utter a phrase, "If it ain't broke, don't fix it." That became the Eleventh Commandment. I fully expected to come into the office one day and see that phrase etched in bronze and hung up on the conference room wall as our mission statement.

My feeling was a little different. "If it ain't broke, you better improve it now." If you don't, you will automatically need a major overhaul sometime sooner than you think. Talk about clashing of cultures!

In the Blazer organization at that time, I couldn't immediately find a soul mate. I had to go it alone. I came up with innovative concepts and jumped some pretty ridiculous hurdles to breathe life into them. But I had one very important thing going for me: clout. The owner of the Trail Blazers wanted me to innovate. He could see that times were quickly changing and that the future of pro sports business was going to be far different than the past. So even though the owner lived in Los Angeles and I had to go through some land mines in the front office in Portland, I knew the owner was supporting me.

Even with that clout, I couldn't have succeeded without recruiting soul mates in the Portland front office. One was a long-time employee who was about to quit over an office squabble. I recruited him to be on my marketing staff. Another was a young woman that we hired as a secretary for the fledgling marketing department. From there, we had our rebel forces.

2: Prepare as if you're going to the Supreme Court to save yourself from the electric chair. Very few bosses, including me, respond well when an employee comes up and wants to send up a trial balloon on a new idea. It usually goes something like this.

> **Employee:** "Hey, I've got a new idea. What do you think about this?" (Insert here a very sketchy description of any new idea that you may have heard lately.)

> **Boss:** (Because the idea is sketchy and not fully fleshed out, the boss will automatically and instinctively see the problems with the new idea.) "Have you thought of this?" (Insert any objection to the idea that the employee floated in front of the boss.)

> **Employee:** "Well, yes, ah . . . ah . . . you see . . . that could be worked out . . . I think. . . ."

> **Boss:** "See ya."

Sure, I might have oversimplified this little discourse. Maybe. I could have put stronger words in the boss's mouth like, "That's a stupid idea," or "That won't work," or "If it ain't broke, don't try to fix it." Any of these phrases would scuttle the idea. Repeat this a few times, and the employee will finally get the message. If the employee stays with the company, that employee will be covered with scar tissue that will always be there to remind the employee of the personal risk of proposing new ideas.

There is an antidote to this: preparation. *Real* preparation. *Written* preparation. Preparation like you're preparing to defend yourself before the Supreme Court. This preparation isn't a trial balloon. This is preparing to get the idea *accepted*.

The written preparation shouldn't be the volumes you may have to prepare for the Supreme Court. In business, *think* those volumes, but prepare a written executive summary that will be six or seven pages. The written executive summary should consist of the following:

Foreword. What are the present conditions of the company in the area that would be affected by the initiation of the new idea. This has to be an unemotional and accurate picture of the situation. If it is not accurate, or if it is skewed by emotion, then your opening premise will be wrong. If the opening premise is wrong, then the solution will be wrong. This is a vital point of the executive summary. The length could vary from one to three pages.

Concept. Concise written statement of what the idea is. (If the foreword is on target, one or two paragraphs or up to one page should suffice here.)

Rationale. Why should the company initiate the idea? What's in it for the company? More sales? More profits? A better workplace? This is a good place to insert budget analysis. How much is it going to cost? How long will it take to get the idea working and money rolling in? Do a cash flow.

Problems. These are the objections you would encounter in trying to sell the idea. There is no sense in trying to skate through without going eyeball-to-eyeball with these objections. After all, your bosses will come up with objections without even thinking. Think of the problems before the boss does. By thinking of objections before the boss does, you're also preparing for how to overcome those objections. How you handle these objections in front of your Supreme Court is the determining factor whether you win or lose. Take several pages in this area if you need to.

Summary. This is a call for approval and a timetable. One or two paragraphs.

One word of warning about this written document: Watch the hype! Go through the document and look at every adjective, adverb, and wildly assertive sentence. Eliminate those that you find. A proposal that is hyped too strongly will lose its credibility. You can use hype, but not in this document. You use it in the next step.

3: Presenting in front of your Supreme Court. You're now prepared to meet the devil face-to-face. This is your chance to be F. Lee Bailey or Johnny Cochran.

If you've recruited a terrorist team for innovation, bring them. However, each person on the team has a designated position. There should be only one captain or "play-by-play person." The others on the team can remain silent, except when it is appropriate for them to contribute as a "color commentator."

At the beginning of your oral presentation, tell your Supreme Court that you have all this in writing. Show them the spiral bound booklet that you've prepared. That's *show*, not *give*. If you give your Supreme Court the booklet, your oral presentation is over, because your Supreme Court will jump ahead, page by page, leaving you mumbling to yourself.

By just showing the booklet, you are underscoring the fact

that the meeting isn't just a trial balloon of "what do you think?" It shows that you are serious. This will set a good stage for you.

Once you've shown your booklet, start innocently enough by restating your foreword. This isn't a reading. This is more conversational, setting up the idea. If you're accurate in relating the present situation, you'll be able to smoothly go to point B, your concept. If you're not accurate in reading the present situation, or you try to skew the situation to fit your concept, be prepared to fight and lose a battle here. By losing here, you lose it all.

Your oral presentation should flow in the same order as your written executive summary, except that you're talking it.

While explaining point B, your concept, you may encounter objections. Try to delay defense of your concept at this stage by saying something like, "I think we have the answer for that, but first let me finish describing this idea."

When you start talking numbers, this is now a good opportunity to open your booklet to the page with the numbers. You use one hand to hold the booklet and one hand and fingers as a pointer to certain numbers. If the numbers are reasonable and not pie-in-the-sky, this should be a smooth part of the presentation.

Your finishing statement is simple. You summarize, you present the booklet to your Supreme Court, and you give the timetable for when you would like to start.

WHEN TO HYPE

It is easier to use hype and emotion during the oral presentation without losing credibility. Here we are talking. It's not being recorded, and it won't be examined and reexamined like a written document.

FACING THE NAYSAYER

I've gone eyeball-to-eyeball against the best naysayers in the world. These people have made a career of saying no. And yet, when I've used the steps described in this chapter, my batting average is about .900. That's nine hits out of ten! I attribute that high batting average to preparation.

There are some things in this world that aren't fair, and after preparing for my Supreme Court, sometimes the oral presentation was too easy. It wasn't even a contest.

It wasn't easy, however, in gathering my terrorist team. Not everybody wants to stand up in front of the Supreme Court and be counted. It also wasn't easy preparing the written document. But once that was done, it was easy to get the approval.

These victories are based on human nature. You see, the Supreme Court is ready, prepared, and poised to say no. The Supreme Court can easily reach back and pull out a few objections. But the Supreme Court is not ready, prepared, and poised to meet a terrorist team that is well prepared. When the Supreme Court throws out an obvious objection, the terrorist team has a decisive and well thought out response. C'mon, that's not fair to the naysayer!

Once I've had some experience with the latest Supreme Court in my life (there are always bosses and then new bosses), there are times that I don't physically write a full proposal. All the work that would go into the proposal—the recruiting of the terrorist team and the preparation of the written document— has been done. What hasn't been done is the actual writing, except for a written spreadsheet of the expected sales gains and costs and a cash-flow spreadsheet for initiating the idea. This shortcut is available only when you have a real working knowledge of the Supreme Court and you're fully prepared.

GETTING FOOLED BY THE SUPREME COURT

Occasionally, I'll think that I really know how my present Supreme Court will react. Sometimes, I'll shortcut my shortcut. Instead of not writing the proposal, I won't recruit for the terrorist team and I won't fully prepare. I'll revert back to a "what do you think" attitude. Wham! The Supreme Court *always*—and I don't think there is ever an exception to the rule—reverts back to slamming the idea before it can be brought to life. And it's an ugly, unmerciful killing. Once the Supreme Court has killed a "what do you think" idea, it's almost impossible to bring it to life. Over the years, I think I've learned this lesson. But occasionally, to save some time, I'll try and float a trial balloon only to see the silo open up and a missile blow that balloon to smithereens. When will I ever learn?

A Simple Test You Can Take

(Fill in the blank.) **"If it ain't broke,**

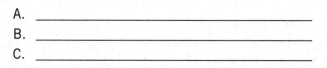

(Fill in the blanks.) **What are the three easy steps to getting an idea approved by management?**

A. _____

B. _____

C. _____

(Multiple choice.) **What's not fair to the naysayer?**

A. A "what do you think" idea?

B. Hype.

C. Preparation.

Answers

1. If you wrote, "don't fix it," you've got some serious problems ahead. Most products today aren't "broken." However, if these products aren't improved, they won't even get the chance to break. The reason is that competitors will come up with better, improved products and steal customers and market share.

    A. Recruit a soul mate.

    B. Prepare as if you're going to the Supreme Court to save yourself from the electric chair.

    C. Presenting in front of your Supreme Court.

I've had people tell me that all that preparation is time-consuming and they would like to skip it.

"How successful are you in getting your ideas approved?" I would always ask.

"Not much, but my boss is really a jerk."

Every boss is a jerk! Heck, I was a jerk when I was the boss. *It all boils down to whether you want your ideas approved.* If you do, you have to prepare for that jerk of a boss. Without the preparation, my feeling is that the person doesn't much want the idea to be approved.

2. We're back to *preparation.* That's the one thing that is not fair to the naysayer. If you just asked, "What do you think?" then it is totally unfair to you and your idea, because it will be lost forever. Hype is also totally unfair to you and your idea. Hype is too easy to shoot down. When hype is shot down, credibility is lost and the idea is shot down.

9. THE JUMP-START GOLDEN RULE

Ground rule #9: Only try to sell a product that the customer wants to buy.

While Billy Ray Bates was the most charismatic player I've ever been associated with, there is one player who is the most uncharismatic. He is far and away the leader in this dubious category. Nobody is in second place. That player is Derrick Coleman.

I had never seen anything like this in all my time in pro sports. Derrick was the star of the New Jersey Nets, and yet the fans hated him more than any other player in the history of the franchise.

If we ran a picture of our star player in a direct response ad for our popular seven-game packages in the newspaper, we wouldn't get one response. When we featured any other player, the phones would ring off the hook. A slew of season ticket holders wrote that they would not renew their season tickets if Derrick was still on the team.

When I left the Nets, I took a golfing vacation in Ireland, and sure enough, Derrick's shadow followed me across the Atlantic. The golf courses in Ireland are the most challenging in the world.

The reason is that weather is 50 percent of the course. Ireland is windy and sometimes rainy, and the wind is a factor on every hole, particularly the links courses that run along the ocean. When I played Ballybunion on the west coast, I had to really plant myself firmly just to putt in the forty-five-mile-an-hour wind.

In the midst of this golf heaven, Derrick Coleman popped up in a most unusual way. We were bracing ourselves against the wind on the tee of a par-three hole. It was 167 yards over a bottomless ravine—167 yards straight into the teeth of the howling wind. My caddie handed me my driver. "I hope it's enough, lad," he said. The caddie should know. He had been caddying at this club for fifty years. Looking at him, he might have started caddying when he was fifty-one.

I didn't want to take a chance with one of my new Titleists, so I rummaged around in my golf bag. I found an old New Jersey Nets ball that was pretty well beat up. The caddie saw the logo on the ball and asked me about the Nets. I told him I used to work for them. He then asked me in an Irish brogue that I could hardly understand, "Is that Derrick Coleman really an arsehole?"

Unbelievable! This caddie knew two NBA players—Michael Jordan and the Darth Vader of the NBA, Derrick Coleman.

I laughed. Then I teed up the Nets ball, drilled it over the ravine in a thirty-mile-an-hour wind, and it dropped six feet from the hole. Birdie putt. And I won another Guinness.

■

We adopted a simple marketing rule when I was with the New Jersey Nets. It was the only marketing rule that we had. It was our key to jump-starting the business operations of the team.

**Only try to sell a product that the
customer wants to buy.**

Our Simple Golden Rule, Part 2

**Try to sell the customer just a little bit more
than they want to buy.**

We translated this as:

- **No crazy up-selling.** This is opposite of the golden rule of many other companies. For example, if a person comes into a car dealership looking for the least expensive car, you know the salesperson will make a pretty good effort in trying to get that person to buy a car that costs twice as much.

  How about insurance? Or computers? Or TV sets? Or office equipment? Overselling with these products seems to be their golden rule; it is their way of life. At the Nets, we didn't focus on overselling.

  If a fan could only afford a seven-game package, we didn't try to sell him or her a full-season forty-one-game package.

  Once we determined what they wanted—and could reasonably afford—we would try to ease that fan up to a *slightly* larger ticket package. It might be an additional three-game package.

  Did we leave money on the table? Probably. But we were also selling satisfaction. If we had hammered a larger sale out of a buyer, let's say to a full-season ticket, our chances for renewal the following season would be slim.

Reasonable down-selling. Down-selling? Isn't this against the American ideal? What crazy talk is this?

Can you imagine a Toyota salesperson recommending *not* to buy the $35,000 Toyota 4Runner, but to buy the $16,000 Tercel instead? If the sales manager found out about that, the salesperson would surely be fired. But think back to our marketing golden rule: Only try to sell a product that the customer wants to buy.

What if the buyer really couldn't afford that $35,000 vehicle? Sure, the buyer might pass the credit check, but the reality of writing checks every month for a car that is too expensive might make that buyer hate the vehicle.

There was a method to our madness to reasonable down-selling. We wanted to retain customers. We were probably the only pro sports team that would mention to season ticket holders in the renewal mailing that they could *downgrade*.

The reason is simple. We knew that things changed in this world, and that a big customer (full season ticket holder) might have to make a smaller investment in tickets. Most teams would look at the season ticket holder who wanted to downgrade as a traitor. Treating a customer as a traitor because they would like to downgrade their commitment usually resulted in losing the buyer altogether. *We didn't want to lose the customer.* If a season ticket holder wanted to buy less, we worked out a ticket package that was right for that buyer. It might have been a twenty-one-game package. Just as we would upgrade people who wanted to go from a smaller ticket package to a full-season ticket, we would be the co-architect with the fan to downgrade that customer's ticket commitment.

- **No bait and switch.** If a company only wanted to buy the scorer's table signage, we didn't try to sell them a radio sponsorship. When working with a sponsor, however, sometimes we could see where a combination sponsorship of scorer's table signage and radio would work better for that sponsor. We'd propose that.

Pretty basic stuff, eh? Except we've all been victims of companies that want to up-sell us to something that we didn't want. Instead of this $400 17" color TV, I know you would really love this 40" $2,000 TV. Instead of this $17,000 car, I know you would really love this $40,000 car. Sometimes, salespeople are successful in selling a product that the customer doesn't really want. What happens then? The salesperson makes a bigger commission, the salesperson's boss is happy, and the company may have lost a customer forever for future purchases.

THAT ISN'T SELLING, IS IT?

"We have a sales staff to sell our tough products," a president of a plastics extrusion company who was sitting next to me on a plane told me.

"You mean to sell products that nobody wants."

"Right . . . well, I wouldn't phrase it that way, but anybody can sell our best products. We wouldn't need salespeople if that is all we sold."

"What would happen if the salespeople spent most of their time selling your best products, the products that the customer most likely wants to buy?" I asked.

"We wouldn't be able to handle it," he said.

My off-the-cuff recommendation to him was pretty simple. Do one of two things:

1. **Fire the sales staff.** Keep a few salespeople to be order takers on the company's best products.

2. **Add a second or third production shift and direct his sales staff to sell products that the customer wanted to buy.**

This jump-start golden rule first started to plant itself in me years ago when I was in college. This little seedling didn't emanate from classes, but from a Ford dealer that I got to know. This was the era of the Mustang and the Falcon. These two cars were forever linked in my mind. The Mustang was the hottest selling car at the time; the Falcon was a dog, and literally an accident waiting to happen.

The dealer told me that he could sell every Mustang he could get his hands on. However, Ford allocated the number of Mustangs (their best product) that he could get from the factory. The allocation was based on how many Falcons he sold (their worst product).

"You mean, you have to sell ten of Ford's worst product to get to sell one of their best?" I asked, full of youthful naiveté.

"Right," he said.

"So, you know that the Falcon is a dog, and that for every one of your customers that are pleased with buying a Mustang, ten of your customers will be ultimately disappointed because high-pressure salesmanship forced a Falcon down their throats."

"Right."

With that marketing philosophy, you could see that Ford itself was an accident waiting to happen. When those Falcon buyers were ready to buy another car in three years or probably less because the car was a dog, they would most likely be looking someplace else. That someplace else happened to be Japan. The American car manufacturers opened the door wide for the Japanese to enter, because they violated the jump-start golden rule. Sure, in the short term it worked. They were able to sell a lot of Falcons, because the dealerships used hammer-

and-tong salesmanship to sell those dogs to get the Mustangs.

What would have happened if that Ford dealer could have sold as many Mustangs as the market would bear, I asked.

"I'd be rich. We wouldn't have to discount like we do with the Falcon. I'd have a lot of really happy customers with Mustangs. My salespeople would build a statue of me and think of me as a saint."

Changing an automotive product line costs a fortune. But could Ford have added more shifts to build Mustangs? Could they have converted assembly lines from Falcon to Mustang? Sure they could. It would have cost a lot, but Ford's benefits would have been equal to the dealers' benefits:

Dealers	Ford
"I'd be rich."	They would have set sales and profitability records.
"I'd have a lot of happy customers."	They would have a lot of happy customers. With a huge bank of happy customers, the door to the U.S. market would have been very narrow for the Japanese.
"My salespeople would build a statue of me and think of me as a saint."	The dealers would build a statue of Henry Ford and think of him as a saint. The car companies and their dealers are usually on an adversarial relationship, because the companies try to force the dealers into selling products that people don't want to buy.

Ford learned their lesson from the Mustang-Falcon marketing strategies. When Ford came out with the Taurus, they did everything possible, and some things that were impossible, to sell as many Tauruses as the customers wanted to buy. The Taurus ended up as the best-selling automobile for five straight years. Dealers didn't have to buy ten latter-day Falcons to sell a

Taurus. If all they wanted to do was sell America's most popular car, they could do that.

There are tremendous benefits to using the jump-start golden rule:

1: Sales will increase. It only makes sense that if you're putting all your energy into products that customers want to buy and very little effort into products that customers don't want to buy, sales will increase significantly.

2: Customers are happy. Customers haven't been mauled to buy bigger and more. They are getting what they want, albeit just a little bit more. A happy customer is much more likely to become the most treasured customer of all—a repeat customer.

3: Can-do swagger. Morale will never be better. By focusing on products that customers want to buy, each person has more confidence, more fun at work, and develops a little swagger in their step. After all, they aren't selling Falcons, they're selling their company's version of the Mustang.

How important is swagger? Well, companies spend thousands of dollars each year to help motivate their workforces through audiotapes and videotapes, books, lectures, placards, you name it. The best motivational device is *success*. If people are selling and producing a product that people want to buy, they're going to feel successful, they are going to feel motivated, they are going to swagger.

YOU WISH THIS COULD HAPPEN TO YOU

What happens when a company runs out of products that the customer wants to buy? This is a pretty good dilemma to be in. There are two good options and one mediocre one:

1: Best option: Produce more of the product that the customer wants to buy. In manufacturing, it is usually possible to make more of a popular product. It might cost a little bit more to make, because suppliers might have to airship parts. But satisfied customers are worth the additional cost of manufacturing.

In some cases, it's not possible to make more popular products. When a concert is sold out, it's sold out. When a Nets' game is sold out, it's sold out. No more people can be shoehorned into the arena. When I was with the Portland Trail Blazers, we solved that problem.

For the eleven years that I was with the Blazers, we sold out the arena for every game. Even though every game was a sellout, some games were bigger than others, and the demand for tickets was greater. We couldn't enlarge the arena for those big games. Instead, we sold additional "tickets" on cable television as pay-per-view. In some instances, the revenue from pay-per-view was greater than the revenue from the gate receipts. Thus, we were able to produce more of the product that the customer wanted to buy.

When we tried to extend that concept to other games—games that were also sold out, but not as high in demand—we failed miserably. In some of these cases, we didn't receive enough revenue from the pay-per-view to cover our production costs.

2: Second best option: Build a waiting list. If additional products that the customer wants to buy can be produced in a reasonable time frame, then make a waiting list and get some financial commitment from the buyer.

If additional products cannot be produced in a reasonable time frame, you could still start a waiting list. But be assured that the longer the time is that the person is on the waiting list, the less likely that person is to eventually buy. Usually, when the person is waiting on the list, other alternatives pop up and that person becomes a buyer someplace else.

3: **Mediocre option: Trying to sell your second-best product.** The second-best product that is similar to the best product might be an acceptable solution to the customer. In many cases, it is not. The customer was thinking about a specific product, and the second-best usually isn't good enough. That customer most likely will look to the competition.

SUCCESS CREATING SUCCESS

At the Nets, we spent all of our energies in trying to sell out games. This started with the games that people most likely would want to go to—the games with the marquee players on the opposing teams. You might think it was easy. It wasn't. If we hadn't committed all of our resources and manpower to selling out our best games, we wouldn't have. A funny thing happened on our way to sellouts. Our attendance picked up in the other games where we weren't even trying.

When the perception started to get around New Jersey that games were selling out, it became socially acceptable for fans to attend our other games. No longer was it an embarrassment to be seen at a Nets game. No longer did fans think of wearing Groucho Marx masks when they went to one of our games. The success of the sold-out games was creating and feeding greater attendance at our other games.

The golden rule? Our people didn't have it tattooed on their chests. It just became a part of their personality, a part of their very being. When we went to league meetings, our people no longer had to slink in through the back door. There was a bit of a swagger as they strutted in the front door.

A Simple Test You Can Take

(Fill in the blanks.) **The golden rule has two parts. What are they?**

A. _____

B. _____

(Fill in the blanks.) **When using the golden rule, at least three important things happen. What are they?**

A. _____

B. _____

C. _____

(Fill in the blank.) **What is the best option for a company when they run out of the product that the customer wants to buy?**

_____

Answers

1. The marketing golden rule is: Only try to sell a product that the customer wants to buy. The second part of the golden rule is: Try to sell the customer just a little bit more than what they want to buy.

A. Sales increase.

B. Customers are happy.

C. Employees will walk with a swagger.

2. Somehow, some way, make more of that product. Two of the most creative acts in business are how to feed an already successful product and how to create more of it. If you're fortunate enough to be in a position to have a product that customers want to buy, but it is sold out, be creative. Think how you can manufacture more of that product.

10. YOU CAN'T JUMP-START FROM AN IVORY TOWER

> *Ground rule #10: Get the feel for jump-start marketing outside the ivory tower.*

We all know that the only thing consistent in this world is change. But sometimes change sneaks up on us.

One change that sneaked up on me is that I'm writing this chapter on my computer on an airplane headed for Hawaii. Just a few years ago, I would be writing this with paper and pen.

In the world of sports we've seen tremendous change. When I was a kid following the Detroit Lions, offensive linemen weighed about 220 pounds. Now they're considered small if they weigh less than 300 pounds. There is one incident in sports, however, that I think illustrates change more than any other.

This one incident involved my dad. As I have written, he was a sportswriter for years in Detroit. If you're not from Detroit, but read the *Sporting News*, you would probably recognize his name, Watson Spoelstra. He also wrote for the *Sporting News* for thirty-some years when it was commonly known as the "baseball bible."

For many of the years when he covered the Tigers, they were lousy. My dad always said that covering a lousy team was more difficult than covering a pennant contender. (Ha! If he thinks covering a lousy team or product is tough, try marketing one.) Anyway, in 1968 a miracle happened. The Tigers won the pennant. That was the year that Denny McLain won thirty-one games during the regular season. McLain was a terrific pitcher, and somewhat of a character, which made great copy. Unfortunately for my dad, the newspapers in Detroit were on strike for almost the entire season. He couldn't write one published word about this terrific team.

The next season, my dad got to write a lot about Denny McLain. He won twenty-four games that season. Then, in the off-season, Denny was suspended by the commissioner of baseball for allegedly hanging around the wrong guys. When I look back, that wasn't so shocking. But what happened the *next* season was.

At the halfway point of the season, Denny was reinstated to pitch. The hope was that his first-half suspension would produce an arm-rested Cy Young pitcher to lead the charge to another pennant.

Denny had pitched three games when he was egged on to pull a prank. His teammates dared him to dump a bucket of water on a writer. Any writer. Who then walks into the Tiger locker room? My dad, of course. And he got the bucket of water.

My dad was wet and angry. After all, he didn't think it was so funny that he had to work the game in a drenched suit. He stormed up to Jim Campbell, the GM of the Tigers, and complained. Campbell reacted swiftly. He suspended Denny the next day for the rest of the season. With the suspension, all hopes of a pennant were gone.

Now, let's look at how that incident underscores change. Name a general manager today in sports who would suspend his star player during a pennant race because of a prank? Remember, Denny had won fifty-five games in the previous two years. Those fifty-five victories would be the equivalent today of suspending your top two starters. Maybe even three starters.

Name a player agent today who would allow his player to be suspended. (Back in Denny's day, there weren't agents.) Name a players' association today that would allow a player to be suspended.

Denny's suspension shows how sports has changed. Agents have become more powerful than team owners. Players' associations have become more powerful than their leagues. Players have become richer and richer. And, of course, as the players became millionaires, marketing people were brought into sports to sell more tickets and pricier sponsorships.

So, I can see that if sports had not changed, I might have ended up marketing a Harley Davidson golf cart.

■

If you were a high-ranking executive at General Motors, you would start your day by being chauffeured to work. You'd then have breakfast on the fourteenth floor, where the chairman and president have offices. If it were howling cold in January and you wanted strawberries with your breakfast, no problem, a bowl of fresh strawberries would be placed in front of you.

While perhaps not as ostentatious, many executives of companies that need a jump-start begin their days in the same pampered way. Instead of being chauffeured, the executive might actually drive. But there would be the priority covered parking spot.

Why not take the bus instead?

I know a president of a Fortune 100 company who did just that. Every day. His name is Ed Gelsthorpe, and he was president of Gillette in the mid-1970s. A chauffeur-driven car was automatically part of the perks for being president of Gillette. And yet, Ed took the bus.

"Why?" I asked him.

"We're in the deodorant business, we're in the shampoo business, we make razor blades, we make pens. These are products purchased by everybody. All day long, I'm around executives that make hundreds of thousands of dollars and are chauffeured to and from work. I need to be around *people*, not just executives. It's not that I will discuss deodorants or razors or shampoo with these people on the bus, but I just need that lifeline to observing people—our customers. I need to hear people—our customers—talk. I need to see them walk, I need to see them tired."

SITTING IN THE FRONT ROW

Once you're an owner or an executive of a pro sports team, you have the clout to sit in the best seat in the house. It might be a luxury suite. It might be preferred seating. It might be the front row. Of all the executives and owners of pro sports teams that I know, each one sits in those choice seats. However, during my twenty years of being an executive with pro sports teams, I followed what I called the "Ed Gelsthorpe Rule." In effect, I rode the bus. I sat in the first row, all right. The first row in the second deck, otherwise known as the cheap seats.

There was one great advantage that I had watching the game from the cheap seats. *I got to hear the fans' reactions.* This was absolutely vital.

By listening and watching up in my perch, the fans told me what they liked and what they didn't like. When I was president of the New Jersey Nets, the fans didn't particularly like our team, but that was to be expected because of the way we played. What I listened and watched for was how they enjoyed the evening, in spite of the team.

What type of reaction was there for the indoor fireworks that we used to add some excitement during the singing of the national anthem? How did the fans like our goofy antics during a time-out? By sitting up in the cheap seats, you would know that our fans loved the sumo racers. These were two college student interns in large padded outfits resembling sumo wrestlers. They would race each other on the floor, bumping into each other and sending each other sprawling. It sounds silly, it was silly, and yet for the fans—and me—it was really fun. Unfortunately, the way the Nets played, the sumos were the highlight of the evening.

By sitting in the choice seats, it's more difficult to get the feel of how the fans feel. The worst place in the arena to get this feel is in the owner's suite. I had, on occasion, sat in the owner's suite. It was terrific. Do you want a hot dog and a Coke? Just get out of your chair and walk a couple of steps to the buffet table and help yourself. While the suite had all the amenities, it was also like watching a game in a cocoon. The suite had large glass windows and two of them would open. Still, the sound of the crowd was severely muffled. Worse, the experience of the fans was shrouded by this cocoon. If you wanted to close a big deal during a basketball game, the suite could be the right environment. However, if you wanted to know how the fans liked various aspects of the game presentation, it would be very difficult to make a judgment from the suite. It would go from difficult to impossible if you wanted to jump-start a team or a company. For instance:

- **Could you jump-start a fast-food franchise if you only ate your meals in finer restaurants?** Sure, you could look at sales numbers, but would you have *the feel?* You could observe focus groups. You could compile research as thick as the Manhattan telephone book. But would you have *the feel* for how your customers responded to a new sandwich you were offering? Of course not.

- **Could you jump-start a group of car dealerships if you never had to make monthly payments on a car or had company cars that were rotated every time the odometer reached 5,000 miles?** Look at the numbers. You'd see how many cars were sold. You'd see which salespeople were leading the pack. But would you have the feel for your customers? Of course not.

- **Could you jump-start a group of gas stations if you never purchased gas because some assistant's responsibility was to always top-off your engine?** What if you never had to arrange for a tune-up or an oil change? Sure, you could study the numbers. You could see how many gallons of gas each station sold, how many tune-ups they did. But would you *feel* what the customer is feeling? Of course not.

- **Could you jump-start a retail store if you never walked the floor, but just stayed rooted in your office?** Would you have the feel for the bulk of your customers? Of course not.

WALKING THE FLOOR

When I was president of the Nets, I was asked to be on the board of directors of a retail chain that had about $3 billion in annual sales. The president of the retail chain "recruited" me, and the chairman took me out to lunch to make the pitch.

While I certainly was honored that they had at least entertained the thought of me joining their board, I was a bit intimidated by their size. All in all, a pro sports team's revenues are in the $50-million range, not the $3-billion range of this chain.

"Why in the world would you want me on your board?" I asked the chairman over lunch. "The Nets are smaller than most of your suppliers. I've never been associated with a retail store . . . "

The chairman was quick. "Our board is mostly financial types. We need marketing. And while you haven't had the classic retail experience, we want a marketer who will think outside 'the box.' You think outside 'the box.'"

I enjoyed being on the board. But after a year and a half, I resigned from the board. I was leaving the Nets and moving back to Portland, Oregon. Of course, I could still have flown in for the quarterly meetings. I still would have received volumes of financial data. But since it was a chain of stores on the East Coast, I couldn't regularly walk the floor of the stores. I couldn't regularly buy things at the stores. While I was on the board, I walked the floor of the stores—and their competitors—at least three times a week. Not coming from a classic retail background, I needed to get the *feel* of retail. The only way that I know how to do that was to go where the customers were. Listen, hear, *feel.*

JUMP-START MARKETING IS JAZZ

Jump-start marketing is not a science. I think it's an art. It's jazz, not a symphony. With a symphony, everybody in the orchestra carefully and painstakingly follows the notes for their instrument. In jazz, there is direction, and I guess that there are rules, but a lot of it is *feel.* Jazz is improvisation. With jazz, every note cannot be captured on paper. The same applies to jump-start marketing. And the origin of *feeling* is never found in the ivory tower.

It will take an effort to get out of the ivory tower. Once you reach a lofty position in a company, the rest of the employees—almost by instinct—will try to paint you into an ivory tower. Here are some of the things that I have done over the years to make sure I didn't get walled into an ivory tower.

1: **Answering my own phone.** I didn't have an executive secretary or an assistant screen my phone calls. I had one simple rule about answering phones.

> If I was in my office and my phone rang, I would answer it. If I wasn't in the office and my phone rang, I wouldn't answer it. My voice-mail message would say, "I'm unable to answer my phone now, but if you leave your name and phone number, I'll call you back within twenty-four hours." Which I did.

By answering my own phone, nobody would screen my calls. I talked to anyone who wanted to talk to me. A lot of times, it was fans, and they were shocked when I picked up my phone. It went something like this:

> "This is Jon Spoelstra," I would say when answering my phone.
> Pause.
> "Uh . . . I would like to speak to Jon Spoelstra . . ." the caller would stammer. Clearly they had been expecting a secretary or somebody else to answer my phone.
> "This is Jon Spoelstra . . . "
> If the fan was calling to complain about something, the venom had quickly evaporated when I had picked up my own phone. And then we would usually have a very constructive conversation.

2: **Taking all the tough complaints.** With any business, it seems that about 3 percent of its customers are real jerks—the customers that the employees love to hate. I call it the "3 percent jerk factor."

While this may seem distasteful, the "3 Percenters" are actually valuable marketing tools. In straight-from-the-hip language, they'll actually tell you what is wrong and what it will take to please them. The remaining 97 percent of the customers usually won't tell you that. If they're dissatisfied, they'll just quietly stop being your customer.

With the Portland Trail Blazers, and then with the New Jersey Nets, I instructed the staff that if any of these 3 Percenters were verbally roughing them up, they should refer the call to me. I couldn't and wouldn't allow myself to miss this type of marketing tool. The conversation would go something like this:

Employee: "Mr. 3 Percenter (our employee would, of course, use the customer's real name), would you like to speak to our president?"

3 Percenter: "Yeah, sure, you just want to get rid of me. Your big-shot president won't take my call."

Employee: "Let me see if he is in. If he is, I'll transfer your call. If he isn't, you'll get his voice mail and he'll personally call you back within twenty-four hours."

(My phone rings.)

Me: "This is Jon Spoelstra."

3 Percenter: "Uh . . . you're the president? Uh. . . ."

The 3 Percenter's venom was usually exhausted by this time. The brunt of the attack had been absorbed by the employee. Rarely would I even get any shrapnel. What I would get is information on how we could improve.

Talking to the 3 Percenters might seem like a cold-shower way of getting out of the ivory tower, but the information they give is valuable stuff. Thank God for the 3 percent jerk factor!

3: No priority parking, no special perks. There weren't any perks as an executive at the Nets, except that the execs got paid more. No numbered parking spots, no nothing. If I wanted tickets to the games, and even though there was a special employee low price, I still had to personally *buy* them—at the same rate as the rest of the employees. Executives paint themselves into an ivory tower when they shower themselves with perks. Isn't it enough to get paid more money without flaunting a bevy of perks in employee faces?

4: Forcing closeness with the customer. In my world, I called this "working the game." Sure, I think every marketing person knows their bigger customers. In my case, I also wanted to know the nameless, faceless customers. These were the thousands upon thousands of fans who attended our games. I couldn't know them all individually, but I could let them paint a mosaic in my mind of what they liked and what they didn't like.

To help this mosaic be created, I occasionally would step forward before a game and act as an usher, handing out our free game program to fans who came through the turnstile. What did that tell me? Well, I found out firsthand that the fans *loved* our free twelve-page program. In fact, about half of the fans would *thank me* for handing them something that could have been just an advertising flyer. I could *feel* that the fans really appreciated the free program. That feeling would transcend to the selling process when we were pitching sponsors for the program.

I've sold tickets in the box office, I've cooked and served hot dogs, and I've passed out programs. After awhile, the mosaic of the nameless, faceless army of customers becomes very clear.

5: Buy your own product. In sports, this means standing in line for a hot dog. Besides sitting in the cheap seats (that I paid for), I always bought food at the concession stands. I'd wait in line like everybody else. I wanted to see how much of the game fans would miss standing in line. I wanted to see how the fans were treated when they bought food and drinks. I wanted to eat what they ate.

Do you buy your own product? If you work for Boeing, that might be a little costly buying a $40 million airplane. But almost everybody else can buy their own product.

Sure, you might get the product for free or at a deep discount. If you want to jump-start a company or a department, dig down and buy your own product. You'll learn so much more about your customers when you become a legit customer. That knowledge will pay huge dividends career-wise, so huge that you can easily buy your own product instead of taking it for free.

6: Direct line to complaints. One sure way of staying in an ivory tower is to shield yourself from customer complaints. At the Nets, we issued an "owner's manual" booklet that was sent to every fan who bought a ticket package. The booklet was only eight pages, featuring answers to problems that may occur in attending a game. For instance, what to do when you lose your tickets or your car won't start in the parking lot. The first two pages of the booklet featured a one-on-one contact with me. On one page was a letter from me asking the fans to either mail or fax any complaints they may have about attending our games. The other page was a form that the fan could use. The faxes came directly into my private fax machine. I read every one of them. I solved very few of the problems or complaints. Instead, I would delegate it to the proper staff person. We had to respond to the fan—with a copy to me—within twenty-four hours. If a solution wasn't possible within twenty-four hours, then we had to give the fan a certain timetable.

The fans that used the one-on-one contact were different from the 3 Percenters. The 3 Percenters would freely pick up the phone and air their complaint. The one-on-one contact made it easy for the regular fan to contact me. Their information was absolutely invaluable.

It was invaluable in helping us improve our customer service. And mostly, it was invaluable in keeping me out of the ivory tower. When you see complaints firsthand every day, it's difficult to hide in that ivory tower.

RIDING THE BUS

When I first started consulting with the Nets, they had never experienced any problems with parking at the arena. The arena's capacity was 20,000 fans. The parking lot could accommodate enough cars for about 15,000 of those fans. Since most of the crowds were 6,000 to 8,000, you always got a great parking spot.

As the Nets attendance started to push upward, we started to have problems in the parking lot. When we started to regularly sell out the arena, we experienced big problems. You see, 5,000 of the fans would have to park over at Giants Stadium. From there, they would have to walk a country mile, take a pedestrian bridge, and then walk some more to the arena. If you took this walk on a cold February night, you probably vowed never to take that walk again. You vowed to stay at home the next time you got the urge to see a basketball game.

We decided to do something crazy. We would provide buses.

Even though the arena kept the parking fees, they didn't feel a responsibility to spend some of that on buses. They told us, "If you want to provide buses, provide them at your own expense. Fans don't complain to us about parking at Giants Stadium when Bruce Springsteen is playing at the Meadowlands Arena."

We weren't the New York Giants, and we weren't Springsteen! Fans of theirs would walk through hell.

When we set up the buses, guess who rode them? If you guessed Jim Lampariello, our exec VP, and myself, you guessed right.

We parked over at Giants Stadium and rode the bus. We wanted to see what type of experience it was for the fans. How easy was it? We came up with a lot of ideas on how to make it even better. But where it really worked for me was that I couldn't ride the bus in an ivory tower.

A Simple Test You Can Take

(Circle the answer.) **Let's look at how many feet you have planted in an ivory tower.**

A. By choice, do you answer your own phone?

Yes   No

B. By choice, do you take some calls from angry customers?

Yes   No

C. By choice, do you avoid priority parking at work?

Yes   No

D. Do you force closeness to the nameless, faceless customers?

Yes   No

E. Do you buy your own product?

Yes   No

F. Do you ever take a bus? Anyplace, anywhere?

Yes   No

Answers

1: Over a couple of beers, I gave this little test to some friends of mine who are in marketing. One of them asked, "Aren't you taking this a little bit far? After all, we've worked for a lot of the things that you now want us to give up."

"Like what?" I asked.

"Well, how about a secretary?"

"I didn't say that you couldn't have a secretary or an assistant. Heck, I've shared one for years. I just asked about whether you answered your own phone or had your secretary screen your calls."

"I could never get anything done if my secretary didn't screen my calls," my friend said.

"Really?" I said. "How many calls do you get from complete strangers? Think of the time that's wasted with phone tag. Think of the time your secretary wastes answering your phone. That must mean you don't have much for your secretary to do."

I believe that. If you have a secretary or assistant answering your phone, try this for just a couple of weeks. Answer your own phone.

You'll find that you can get a lot more done and that you'll keep each phone call shorter. You'll also find out that your assistant has loads of time to do *more*. That's why I've never had a full-time secretary. I can never find enough things for that person to do!

"Well, what about taking angry calls from customers?" another friend asked. "That's what we have a customer service department for."

This one is a tough one for me to answer. After all, who in the world really *likes* to talk to angry customers. But this is what I said, "My feeling is that you learn just too much about your product and how to market it from angry customers not to talk to them. Don't become your customer service department, but *try it*. Talk to angry customers every once in awhile. Your marketing skills will feel the difference."

Another friend said, "Our company assigns parking for us."

"For *everybody* in the company?" I asked.

"No, of course not. Just the executives."

"You're closer to your office, right?"

"Right."

"What would happen," I asked, "if you *didn't* park in your assigned spot. Would you get fired?"

"Of course not."

"So, *try it* for a couple of weeks. You'll enjoy the walk . . . "

"And you sure need it," another friend said, laughing. "When I walk from an unassigned spot, it gives me a chance to review quickly the things I've got to do for the day."

"Just *try it*," I said. "Try it as a little experiment."

"Okay, I'll try it," my friend said. "But buying your own product is a joke. Jon, remember, I work for a car company. I get a loaner car every three months. If I bought my own product, it would cost me $30,000!"

"What does your car cost your customer? $30,000? Find out what it's like to buy a car, to pay monthly for one, to get your oil changed, to get a dent in your fender fixed."

"That just costs too much," my friend said.

"Does it cost less for your customer?"

Everybody else at the table said that our friend should buy his own car. Of course, all but our friend didn't work for a car company. We had to pay for our own cars, we had to pay for our own repairs. We probably knew more about owning and caring for a car than our friend who marketed cars for a living.

"Well, Jon, to your last question," another friend said, "I do take the bus."

"You do?" I said, surprised.

"Yeah, I've got a Hertz Gold Card. I take the Hertz bus at airports and they drive me right to my rental car."

Now to *your* answers to the simple test you took.

# of yeses   Comment

6   You don't even have one toe planted in an ivory tower. You're a model candidate to make jump-start marketing really work.

4–5 So, you might have half a foot in an ivory tower. Not bad. Just inch that foot back a little. A little more and your foot is out of the ivory tower.

2–3 Which way are you headed? Are you headed toward the ivory tower or out of it? If you're heading into it, your marketing skills will erode. Is the ivory tower worth it? If you answered yes to this question, then you flunk the test.

1   Your marketing skills could be suffering because you're pretty well into the ivory tower. C'mon, turn around and just walk right out of that tower. Go ahead, try it . . .

0   Are you in marketing or finance?

11. MARKETING TO A SEGMENT OF ONE

Ground rule #11: Only target people who are interested in your product.

Most pro athletes don't know how they got to the big leagues. They might tell you it was through hard work. Bull. There are thousands of high school athletes who work far harder than a pro. But those overachieving high school athletes don't have the one thing that the pro athlete has: mind-boggling athletic ability. This ability wasn't developed—it started the day they were born.

God reached down out of the sky and touched the little body of a baby that would someday be a pro athlete. That touch helped make that baby's body grow to 7' tall with tremendous coordination. Or God touched his legs to help him run a 4.2 in the forty-yard dash or touched his arm so that he could throw a ninety-five-mile-an-hour fastball.

A lot of times, God didn't reach up and touch the baby's head. I know of a player who is making close to $4 million a year, and he spends every nickel of it. Year after year. Not on investments, but on *stuff.* You have to work to do that! If you don't think you have to work at it, consider this. How many new Mercedeses and new houses do you have to buy and keep each year to spend your $4 million? Unfortunately, the day this player retires will be the day he is broke.

On a rare occasion, God will touch both the body *and* the head. And then God will turn and touch the parents. On June 22, 1962, He embraced a little baby in Houston, Texas. The name on the baby's crib was Clyde Drexler.

You're familiar, of course, with Clyde. A marvelous athlete who electrified fans at the University of Houston as the leader of Phi Slamma Jamma. He later became a member of the Dream Team in the 1992 Olympics. He won an NBA title with the Houston Rockets in 1995. But of all my memories of Clyde's athletic prowess, one memory that wasn't athletic stands above all.

When I was general manager of the Portland Trail Blazers, occasionally we would have a player over for dinner. One night, Clyde joined us for dinner. Two days later, my wife received a thank-you note from Clyde. We were stunned! Pro athletes don't think in terms of thank-you notes. Certainly, it was a small gesture, but it had a huge impact on us. We all know God touched Clyde's body when he was a baby. My wife and I know He touched his head and Clyde's parents.

■

When I was on that private island in Japan, the phone rang in my suite early one morning. As I tried to snap awake, I thought the ringing phone was one of my Japanese hosts. Instead, it was the president of a major performing arts center in the United States. Somehow, he had tracked me down. If my friend ever left the performing arts business and got into tracking, pity the fugitive who is trying to disappear.

I mumbled a hello.

"Did I wake you?" he asked.

"No, I had to get up to answer the phone, anyway."

My friend apologized for tracking me down and calling me so early. It was actually earlier than he had thought, but he just wanted a *quick* opinion. They were on the verge of hiring a VP-marketing for the performing arts center. He was down to three candidates.

"What would you look for?" he asked.

Sleep. That's what I would look for. There was a pause on the phone as I thought of a more polite and meaningful answer.

"One person is very impressive," my friend said. "She has prepared some really beautiful brochures and mailing pieces for another performing arts center. The best I have ever seen."

My head was clearing a bit.

"That might not impress me," I said. "Yes, it's important, but what is more important, does that person know how to put those expensive brochures into the hands of the right people?"

There was a pause at his end of the line.

"I would really question deeply each candidate's understanding on database marketing," I said. "After all, brochures for performing arts centers are usually really expensive pieces. Your customers are usually very upscale. Sending one of those to a person that is not interested in the arts would cost about $4. Sending those brochures to 30,000 people that are not interested in the arts would cost $120,000. Find the person that knows how to market to a segment of one. So I would ask each candidate two things when they show you the brochures that they have done."

"What are those two things?" my friend asked.

"Call me back in four hours and I'll tell you."

TWO QUESTIONS TO MARKETING TO
A SEGMENT OF ONE

Later that morning, with my second cup of coffee of the day in hand, I explained the two things I would ask for:

Question #1: "What's the ratio?" After looking at the beautiful brochures, I suggested that my friend ask how many were printed and how much they cost to print. He would then ask, "How much revenue did these brochures bring in?"

If the candidate didn't have an answer, or if it was vague, then my friend wouldn't have to ask the second question. He would just thank the candidate and say something polite as the person leaves.

The ratio that I was referring to is an easy one. For every dollar put into a project (in this case, brochures for a performing arts center), how much revenue came in *directly* because of the brochure? If it wasn't measurable, why do the brochure in the first place? I assume that the purpose of mailing brochures is sales. If it is sales, then the ratio is the most accurate and telling way to measure the effectiveness: How much did you spend and how much did you receive?

The answer isn't in percentages. It's in *dollars*.

This type of measurement makes sense to me. We're talking *dollars*—dollar income in relationship to expenses—instead of meaningless percentages.

$$\frac{\underline{Revenue}}{Cost} = Ratio$$

For a brochure mailed to a segment of people that had somehow indicated they were interested in the brochure's product, the ratio would look like this:

$$\frac{\$300,000}{\$35,000} = \$8.57$$

Thus, for every dollar spent on printing and mailing that brochure, the company received $8.57 back. Not bad.

Occasionally, people would ask me what our percentage of response for a *Nets Ticket Catalog* was. I would answer, "I have no idea. The ratio, however, was $10." This meant for every dollar that we had spent in preparing, printing, and mailing the catalog, we would receive $10 back.

Measuring the percent of response tends to be meaningless. For instance, the lower the product price is, the higher your response rate could be. But if you received 100 percent response for a fifty-cent item, you'd lose big.

Here's why you'd lose big: Suppose it costs seventy cents to prepare, print, and mail your offer. Even with a 100 percent response on the fifty-cent item, you'd be losing twenty cents on every order. And that doesn't even count your cost of product. The ratio would be minus seventy-one cents. For every dollar spent in marketing the product, you would get back 71¢.

$$\frac{Revenue\ (50¢)}{Cost\ (70¢)} = Ratio\ (-71¢)$$

Even though the percentage rate of response was phenomenal (100 percent), if you sent out a large mailing, you could go bankrupt in minutes.

On the other hand, what happens when you get an awful percentage response? Let's say 1 percent of 1 percent. That would look like .0001 percent.

If you're selling a $1 million item, that awful percentage response may not be so bad. For instance, a .0001 percent of a mailing of 1 million names would bring 100 buyers. Let's look at this ratio:

Revenue $100,000,000
(100 buyers at $1,000,000 each) = Ratio ($142.85)
Cost ($700,000)

If the candidate for the performing arts center job didn't know how to do that type of simple math, then my feeling was that that person shouldn't be a candidate for VP-marketing. If that type of person got the job, there would probably be a lot of thrashing and flailing in the marketplace—probably all logically thought out. Tens of thousands of dollars would be spent. The image of the performing arts center would certainly be enhanced with a fine glossy mailing, but without knowing the ratio, they could be spending themselves to oblivion. Then that company would soon become a candidate itself—for jump-start marketing.

Question #2: "What lists did you use to mail the brochures?"
I recommended to my friend to listen very carefully to this answer.

"The answer," I said, "is going to tell you if the candidate knows how to market to a segment of one."

"How do you mean?" my friend asked.

"The candidate knows how to market to a segment of one if the list used to mail brochures is a list of people that have somehow indicated an interest in the performing arts."

I gave my friend examples on how we assembled a list of 75,000 names who were people interested in the Nets or the NBA. Those 75,000 names were *our* segment of one.

The common demographic in that list wasn't age and it wasn't income level. It was that these 75,000 people had somehow shown an interest in the Nets and the NBA. And we had captured those names.

MARKETING TO A SEGMENT OF ONE?

How can this be?

Aren't we taught to put people in demographic groupings? Nielsen ratings certainly do. They group people into broad age brackets like eighteen to fifty-four. Eighteen to fifty-four? How silly is that? Which eighteen-year-old should really be grouped with a fifty-four-year-old? But, we're told, that's what marketing is all about. Grouping people into common or semi-common characteristics and then selling them something.

As you know by now, I believe first in putting people into just one segment. That one segment is the people who you know are interested in your product.

When a company buys a list based on a demographic profile, the company really doesn't *know* that the people on that list are interested in the company's product. Because the demographic profile on the list may be close to the demographic of their customers, the company may *think* that these prospects are interested, but they won't know until they put the offer in the mail. Because they *think* the list could be highly productive, the company may spend themselves to oblivion finding out. This leads to the one and only rule.

1: **Test, test and test some more.** A friend of mine who was a real estate agent used a version of the quick-fix silver bullet. This was a simple program, almost stupid.

My friend sent out greeting cards to his friends and past clients. These weren't the normal greeting cards that you would buy in a store. My friend created these cards himself. These four-color, humorous cards reminded his friends that he was always on the lookout for referrals—people *thinking* about buying or selling a house. This gentle little nudge that the cards provided produced a ton of referrals.

Since this worked for him, he thought these cards would work for any realtor. "Every real estate agent in the country should have these cards," my friend told me. I agreed.

"These cards are so good, I'm going to send a brochure to every real estate agent in the country," he said. I disagreed.

I told him to test. To buy 1,000 names and try it.

"But there are 700,000 real estate agents out there. Why test 1,000?"

He ran off and raised some money for this project. He couldn't raise enough money to reach every real estate agent in the country, so he mailed flyers to real estate agents in thirteen Western states. He got orders. Not enough orders, however, to cover his costs. He almost spent himself into oblivion.

On the brink of oblivion, my friend came over to my house one night. We worked on his flyer. We developed two versions. One version had a terrific, unbelievable money-back guarantee. The other had a normal watered-down guarantee. I recommended that he try each version to a test base of only 1,000 realtors.

"One thousand realtors will tell you whether you have a product or not and how you should approach the rest," I said. "The cost to reach one thousand realtors was only $500. That's not spending yourself into oblivion."

The version with the great guarantee got grand-slam home-run results. It produced about $7,500 in sales. That's a $15-to-$1 ratio! With that type of return, he could keep on sending out flyers.

DON'T BECOME A MISSIONARY

Using lists to ferret out the names of people who are interested in your product is expensive. Once you have that information, though, that becomes your segment of one base list. With that segment of one base list, you can divide that list into sub-segments. With the New Jersey Nets, we built a list of 75,000 names. The sub-segments were comprised of buyers and nonbuyers. The buyers were people who had purchased season tickets, mini-plan ticket packages, group tickets, single games, etc. The nonbuyers were people who had entered a Nets contest, called in for a pocket schedule, kids who had written players, etc. The buyer and nonbuyer sub-segments all had one thing in common: They had exhibited an interest in our team. Age and income weren't the demographics that identified our segments. The demographic that we were interested in was the level of their interest in our product. This level of interest is measured by how many tickets they had purchased.

HOW WOULD YOU TALK TO A FRIEND?

You have something in common with the person who has somehow identified themselves as liking your product. That thing in common is that you *both* like your product. That's enough to build a friendship on. If you are indeed a friend of that prospect, treat them like a friend, talk to them as a friend.

That's what I recommended for the Los Angeles Clippers. After I left the New Jersey Nets, the Clippers asked if I would consult for them. The futility of the Clippers on the basketball court was almost a mirror of the Nets. On the business end, the Clippers had taken the Nets' previous position of being last in the NBA in gate receipts. Certainly, they had the potential of being last in gate receipts as many consecutive years as the Nets had.

One of the first assignments was to help them retrieve some of their lost fans. In an effort to boost their attendance, they had moved eight of their home games to Anaheim. While Anaheim is only about twenty-five miles away from their normal home arena, the Sports Arena, rush-hour traffic in LA practically makes it a different time zone. People in Anaheim thought of going to the Sports Arena as often as they thought of going to North Dakota.

The games in Anaheim were popular in the first year. In fact, they sold out all eight games. Most of the fans purchased a season ticket—which was only eight games instead of the usual forty-one.

With these new fans, the Clippers didn't exactly make a good first impression. They lost six of their first seven games by big margins. They finally won a second game at Anaheim, the last one. As a result, the renewal for the games the next season was an astoundingly low 30 percent.

The Clippers had sent nice colorful brochures in the renewal process, all touting a new, exciting, and winning team. After a couple of mailings of beautiful stuff, I recommended that they just write a plain letter as if they were writing it to a friend. Forget the brochure. Forget the hype. Just write a nice, friendly letter. Here's the letter that I recommended:

Mr. Joe Ex-Fan
President
XYZ Company
121 Orange Street
Tustin, CA

Dear Joe:

Talk about putting a wrong foot forward!
As you can guess, we wanted to make a good impression on

you in our inaugural games at the Pond last year. Obviously, we didn't.

With your eight-game package last year, we won only two games.

Well, Joe, this year we do have a better and more exciting team. And, *I'll guarantee that you'll enjoy our games at the Pond.* This isn't an idle guarantee. I'm going to put our money where my mouth is.

We now have a five-game package at the Pond that I think you'll really enjoy.

If you don't enjoy the first game of the five-game package, return the tickets to the remaining four games and you get *100 percent* of your money back for your entire purchase. That's for all five games including the game you attended.

Your enjoyment isn't based on us winning or losing that first game. *This guarantee is based on your enjoyment, and you are the sole judge and jury to that.* Heck, even if you don't like the way I comb my hair, you can get your money back!

There are some terrific advantages for you to buy this five-game ticket package . . . (The next page listed the advantages.)

Best regards,
Andy Roeser
Executive Vice President
LA Clippers

Does it sound like Andy, the exec-VP of the Clippers, was a friend of Joe, the president of XYZ Company? Sure it does. Even though the letter was sent to 3,500 fans who did not renew the Clippers ticket package for Anaheim, each letter sounded like it was written to one person. *Marketing to a segment of one.*

I think this letter is more believable than a brochure, because, at the top of the letter, Andy had admitted that they had had a lousy record in Anaheim. Most teams would never want to admit that they were lousy, but unfortunately the Clippers couldn't hide that fact from last year's buyers at Anaheim. Since we can't hide it, we might as well lead off with it. It brings credibility. It's how you would write a letter to a friend. The response to this letter was greater than the fancy brochures that were sent.

In chapter 4, I wrote about a car dealer sending a letter to a customer whose car was purchased two and a half years before from the same dealer. Usually, a dealer's concept of a letter is a postcard that says it's time for a tune-up. But that type of post-card isn't communication to a *friend*. It would be much more effective for that dealer to send his friend a letter like this:

Dear Jon:

I shouldn't be sending you this letter at this time. After all, you bought a car from me about two and a half years ago, and you're probably not ready for a new one.

However, the features of *FastCar* are so unique that I thought you'd want to know. There are three things I think you'll like about the new *FastCar* . . .

(The dealer would briefly list the benefits and then invite the person to test drive *FastCar.* Each letter would be individually signed by the dealer.)

A while ago, I bought a CD-ROM for my computer that had all of the *Time* magazines in the history of the world squeezed onto that little disk. Like most computer programs, there was a registration card. Or you could register electronically through a phone modem.

I really enjoyed zipping in and out of all these *Time* magazines. I looked at the covers, searched for stories, saw decades fly beneath my finger tips. As much fun as it was, there was one thing that didn't happen. I didn't get a letter from the publisher of *Time*.

A few days after I had electronically registered the computer program, I *should* have received a letter from the publisher. Since both of us had probably surfed all those *Time* magazines, we had something in common. The publisher's letter could have looked like this:

Dear Jon:

I hope you have enjoyed *Time* magazine's CD-ROM as much as I have.

There are a couple of things that are really intriguing about the program:

- (One neat idea about the program.)
- (A second neat idea about the program.)

I checked to see if you've been enjoying *Time* week after week, and Jon, I couldn't find you on our computer.

However, I would like to make you a special offer. You've got all of the past *Time* magazines, why not get all the future ones, too?

Here's the deal . . .

Best regards,
Publisher of Time

A letter like that would sound like the publisher was a friend of mine. Which list do you think would have a higher response rate? A general list or a list of people who had purchased the *Time* magazine CD-ROM? I don't have the answer, but you would think that it would have to be the list where you sent a letter to your friends.

A Simple Test You Can Take

(Fill in the blanks.) **What is "the ratio?"**

$$\underline{\hspace{2cm}} \div \underline{\hspace{2cm}} = \text{Ratio}$$

(Fill in the blank.) **What is a segment of one?**

_____

(Multiple choice.) **How would you talk to a person in your segment of one?**

    A. As just another number among thousands.
    B. As a friend.
    C. Just like anybody else.

Answers

1: $\dfrac{\text{Revenue}}{\text{Cost}} = \text{Ratio}$

2: People who have exhibited an interest in your product. These people could be current buyers, people who have requested information from you, or people who entered a sweepstakes that you ran.

If the names came through a sweepstakes, you could get fooled. I'll give you an example. Let's say you own a chain of office supply stores. You decide to run a sweepstakes in the newspaper. If the prize of the sweepstakes is $100 million (you're a *very* successful chain), you're going to get a lot of people who enter the contest who don't care the slightest about you and your stores. They want the $100 million.

However, if the prize was an expensive color copier, then those names would most likely be good names for your segment of one. Those names have exhibited an interest in your product: the color copier that you also sell.

3: As a friend. I'm always surprised that when I have somehow indicated to a company that I am a friend, they communicated with me as if I were a stranger.

In this age of technology, it's easier than ever before to communicate with friends. In pro sports, why do letters for renewing season tickets start out "Dear Season Ticket Holder"? Is that the way to address a friend?

Why do so many letters to customers sound like they were written by an accountant? Heck, when my accountant drops me a personal note, he doesn't sound like an accountant. He sounds like a friend.

12. CHEAP IS GOOD, BUT FREE IS BETTER

*Ground rule #12: Don't let research
make the decision for you.*

To get approval to change the name of the New Jersey Nets to the
Swamp Dragons, we needed to convince the executive committee
of the NBA. The executive committee was comprised of the most
powerful owners.

If they approved, I was told that the vote for the rest of the
league was pretty much a rubber-stamp vote. In fact, the rest of
the league had never voted against the wishes of the executive
committee.

The executive committee was chaired by Jerry Colangelo, president and managing partner of the Phoenix Suns. After I had
made the presentation to the group, Colangelo didn't seem
impressed with the wild idea of changing our name to the Swamp
Dragons.

"Have you done research on this?" he asked. "Have you polled
your fans? Have you had focus groups with your fans?"

I respect Colangelo. In a period of about twenty-five years, he
had gone from promotions director of the Chicago Bulls to part-

owner of a sports empire, which included the Phoenix Suns, out there in the Arizona desert. Besides running the Suns, he put together the investors that bought a major league expansion team and he lured the Winnipeg Jets to play in the America West Arena. In putting this empire together, I imagine that Colangelo had commissioned a lot of research to support what he wanted to do. While I respect Colangelo, I didn't respect his thoughts on research for a name change.

"No," I answered.

I could tell that he was surprised.

"I don't believe in that type of research," I added.

"Could you explain that to us?"

"I think so. I don't think that research is that valid for things that have *not* happened. People haven't *lived* it yet. People would just give a knee-jerk reaction, generally negative. Research is valid for asking about how somebody enjoyed something, but not for something in the future. The only way you can research something like this is to talk to a lot of people that you respect, just do it, and then see what happens."

No comment from Colangelo.

I then gave an example.

"When Disney bought an expansion hockey team, they named it the Mighty Ducks," I said. "They were crucified by the media and by their potential fans." I brought out some of the newspaper articles from Los Angeles. Before I could read from some of the stories that had lampooned Disney, another owner spoke up. It was the owner of the Detroit Pistons, Bill Davidson.

"Jon's absolutely right," the Pistons owner said. "When we named our new arena the Palace, the media and the fans were in an uproar. They thought it was a disgrace. If we had done a polling of our fans, we would be called something like Detroit Piston Arena."

I was surprised by Davidson's remarks. I had always thought that the Palace was a fabulous name for an arena. I had never known about the negative media.

Jerry Buss, the owner of the Los Angeles Lakers, spoke next. "The media will hate the name for a few days, and the kids will buy all the Swamp Dragons licensed products. I think this is a brilliant thing to do. I wish we could do it."

The Pistons owner spoke up again. "This is too important of a decision to let the fans vote on it. Jon's right, they haven't *lived* it. Like naming the Palace, they won't have an opinion on it until they've fully experienced it. Research could just fool you."

I liked that line: Research could just fool you.

So I came up with some personal guidelines where research could only help you market a product. This won't be appreciated by the big research companies, because this research is free. Cheap is good, but free is better.

■

I hate Sunday night sporting events. Like me, I think most people would prefer to be at home on Sunday night.

When I was with the Portland Trail Blazers, we would usually have about 40 percent of our home games on Sunday nights. That meant I would hate to go to about 40 percent of our games. Eventually, our fans would realize that they hated it also, and our sellout string of games would end.

I couldn't get the NBA to give us fewer Sunday night games. So I did a little research.

Since we had to have a lot of Sunday night games, how could we make it better? We didn't ask the general public. We asked our season ticket holders. In our season ticket renewal mailing, we put a questionnaire on the invoice.

"At what time would you like our Sunday night games to start?" *(Check one.)*

4:00 P.M.
5:00 P.M.
6:00 P.M.
7:00 P.M.
7:30 P.M.

Our usual start time had been 7:30 P.M. For the Sunday night games, over 75 percent of the fans wanted 5:00 P.M. With a 5:00 P.M. start time, the fans would be home by about 7:30 P.M. It seemed like they also hated Sunday night games. Easily, confidently, swiftly, we changed the start time to 5:00 P.M.

This is the type of area where I feel research can help: researching your current customers on specific points about the product or the experience. The great thing about this type of research is that it is free. We didn't even have to pay for postage. This little piece of research was included in our season ticket renewal letter.

LETTING RESEARCH TAKE THE BLAME

In Japan, many decisions are made by a committee. The best part of "decision by committee" is that when things don't work out as planned no one can be individually blamed. We have taken that system a few steps further. At many companies, particularly the megacorporations, they let research make the decision for the committee.

The classic case of letting research make the decision is Coca-Cola. As we all know, Coke was concerned about how Pepsi

Cola was winning the market share among young people. Coke didn't think that Pepsi's victory over youth was marketing; Coke thought that it was in the product's *formula*. So Coke decided to reformulate. They would make Coke sweeter, thinking that this would better appeal to the palate of young people. Millions of dollars were spent on research. There were hundreds of thousands of blind taste tests. You know, "Drink from this cup, then drink from that cup. Which one do you like best?"

All the research showed that consumers preferred the taste of the new Coke. The research was wrong. Yes, in the blind taste tests, people said that they liked "cup A" over "cup B." However, people weren't buying cup A or cup B. When people found out what was in cup A and cup B, they loudly said that they preferred their old Coke, not the new Coke.

Coca-Cola responded quickly to the outraged Coke drinkers of the world. They came back with the original formula and named it Classic Coke. It was appropriately named. It was a classic mistake of letting research fool you.

AVOIDING GETTING FOOLED BY RESEARCH

During all those taste tests, do you think that the chairman of Coca-Cola went into a supermarket and watched people choose a soft drink? For the moment, let's assume that he did indeed watch.

What he would be looking for would be consumers who walked directly past any special price offers from Pepsi or other competitors. He would be looking for people who zeroed in on the Coke display as if they were human heat-seeking missiles. He would watch these people lift a few six-packs of Coke and put them into their shopping cart.

"Excuse me," the Coke chairman would ask the Coke buyer,

"but we're doing some research. I'll trade you one Pepsi six-pack and a dollar for each one of your Coke six-packs."

That, of course, would surprise the shopper. The Coke chairman might have to repeat the offer.

"No thanks, I'll keep my Coke," the Coke shopper would most likely say.

"Okay, I'll give you two Pepsi six-packs for each of your Coke six-packs."

"No."

"Okay, I'll give you three Pepsi six-packs for each of your Coke six-packs."

The Coke chairman wouldn't have to keep notes. The chairman would see everything on the Coke shoppers' faces. The shoppers' faces would create a mosaic that the Coke chairman would never forget.

Why in the world should the Coke chairman have done this? Why not outsource this to a big research firm? Well, the decision to change Coke's formula involved hundreds of millions of dollars. The decision wasn't made at the lower levels. It was made in the chairman's office. A little bit of free research could have been a lot more valuable than the hundreds of thousands of taste tests.

There could have been a better way to battle Pepsi. Coke has tremendous marketing muscle. Their distribution channels are second to none. That muscle and distribution strength could have been used to create a new cola product that would have been targeted directly at Pepsi. Then, let the research dollars flow. "Drink from this cup, now drink from that cup? Which one do you like best?"

Research can be useful in measuring experiences or opinions of your or somebody else's customers. In the case of the starting time for the Blazers Sunday night games, our season ticket holders had experiences of attending games. Most of them had been attending a lot of games for a lot of years. They understood start times. They could visualize what each start time meant to them. These were valid opinions. The vote was overwhelmingly for a 5:00 P.M. start time. If it had been a close vote, we wouldn't have changed.

Invalid research would have been to ask people who didn't go to any Blazer games. The research could look something like this: If you were going to go to a Blazers game on Sunday night, what start time would you prefer? My feeling is that these people wouldn't have valid opinions, since they weren't regularly experiencing Blazers games.

WHERE RESEARCH CAN BE USEFUL

From reading the chapter, you probably get the idea that I'm not a big fan of research. Well, you're right and you're wrong. I'm a big fan of research in two areas:

1: Using research to sell something: People that you're selling something to may need research to make a decision.

While this may be research, I look at it more as a marketing tool. Here, you're going to have to spend money. You won't be able to get by with just building a "personal mosaic" of how your customer feels about your product. You have to go out and buy credibility from a research firm.

Here's where research can be an important tool to helping sell something:

- **Getting a loan.** You're trying to get a business loan. You have to prove to the banker that this is a low-risk loan. To prove your point and get the loan, research could provide the needed credibility.

- **Getting investors.** I imagine that Jerry Colangelo used piles of research to prove that a major league baseball team or NHL team would be a terrific investment in the Phoenix area.

- **Selling a product.** Good examples of this are radio and TV stations. They generally need ratings research to prove to a media buyer that the station's audience is perfect for that advertiser.

When it comes to selling something to somebody, research can add credibility. It can also add expense. But I look at that expense as a marketing expense, and the "cheap is good, but free is better" doesn't apply here.

2: **Research and development.** I'm a huge fan of research and development. This is basically spending the resources to come up with new products or improve existing ones. The moniker "research and development" might be a little lofty for me— I visualize scientists with thick eyeglasses wearing lab coats— but the concept of a company always spending time and money to come up with new products and improve their existing products is essential to feeding jump-start marketing. I'd prefer to call such a department the "fun-and-games" department. That moniker may be too frivolous to many. After all, what if you're a big shot for an insurance company or oil refinery, and your title is vice president of fun and games? That doesn't sound very prestigious. But when you scrape away all the mystique of research and development, it *is* fun and games.

Fun-and-Games Department (aka Research and Development)

When we were kids, it was fun to learn new puzzles. For adults, developing new products or improving existing products is also fun. The games part is the positioning of this new product.

When is a company too small to spend money and time on a fun-and-games department (or, if you prefer, research and development)? No company is too small. A one-person company may not be able to have a fun-and-games department, but part of the brain of that one person has to be partitioned off to developing new products or improving existing ones.

WHERE RESEARCH CAN FOOL YOU

Research can fool you all the time.

It can particularly fool you when major decisions are to be made. With major decisions—where somebody has to be sold on something—big professional research firms are brought in for credibility. A ton of money is spent. It's understandable that more credibility is given to these huge research reports than to the free research.

When all the big research dollars have been spent, however, it's time for some free research before the final decision is made. Free research is going to your customers and talking to them one-to-one. If you talk to enough of them, you'll get that very clear mosaic of what your customers are *feeling*. This type of research will not fool you.

A Simple Test You Can Take

(Fill in the blanks.) **In what two areas can research be useful?**

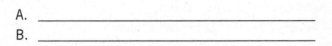

A. _____

B. _____

(Multiple choice.) **How important is your fun-and-games department?**

    A. Very important.
    B. Important.
    C. Not very important.
    D. We don't have one.

Answers

1. A. Using research to try to sell something to somebody.
   B. Research and development.

2. To keep jump-start marketing going, your answer here should be (A). It's absolutely essential to come up with new products or improve existing products.

In pro sports, it could be argued that *every* pro team has an R&D department. That would be their player personnel department, which is usually headed by the general manager. After all, the GM is responsible for improving the team (the product) through the draft, trades, or a new coach.

However, on the business side of sports, where new products are unique ticket packages or new forms of sponsorship, there are only two pro sports teams that I know of that have had a research-and-development department: the Portland Trail Blazers and the New Jersey Nets.

Because of the fun-and-games department, both teams have had more breakthrough marketing products than any other team. Was it just by accident or dumb luck? Hardly. New products and improvement of existing products were the fun-and-games department's reason for existing.

The actual fun-and-games department wasn't big. In each case, it was one person plus anybody else they could temporarily steal from another department. The product concepts were usually developed under the guidelines of chapter 7 (Innovate, Innovate, Innovate). The director of the fun-and-games department then did everything that was necessary to shepherd that new product to the marketplace.

13. I'LL BE YOUR FRIEND FOR ANOTHER YEAR

Ground rule #13: Make your client a bona fide, real-life hero.

I've said to people that what I like about being in pro sports is that it means *nothing*. In sports, you don't pollute the rivers, the fields, or the skies like some companies do. You don't manufacture anything tangible. You just pay young men an illogical amount of money to play games in front of people.

There is a redeeming factor, of course, about working in pro sports. Pro sports provide a relief for individuals from the problems of the world. This relief is more encompassing than the salve generated in other entertainment areas like the movies or concerts.

A movie or a concert lasts for a couple of hours and there is no ongoing emotional attachment. With pro sports, the emotional attachment is yearlong. The season lasts about seven months, then there's the off-season. A fan can be mentally entrenched with his/her team for twelve months out of the year, year after year, decade after decade.

Some may say that this entrenchment is not good. Yes, there

are some fans whose favorite team is more important to them than their jobs or even their family. That, of course, is extreme. I guess you'd call that a *fana*tic.

For most fans, the teams provide a mental ballpark to which they can escape for a short time each day. Sometimes, a fan will try to take this mental ballpark with them to the next life.

In the early 1980s, Sue Miller, my marketing assistant at the Portland Trail Blazers, came into my office with an unusual request from such a fan. "I got a call from a woman that asked where she could buy a copy of the 'Blazer Music,'" Sue said. The "Blazer Music" Sue was referring to was the music that we played at the beginning of our radio broadcasts.

The music was semi-original. Several years before, we had gone to a sound studio and listened to hundreds of instrumental songs in the sound studio's library, trying to find a piece we thought was right for the Blazers. Instead of picking one piece of music, we selected about six or seven. We took what we liked from each piece and edited them together for our own distinctive sound. We had a drum roll from one piece of music, trumpets from another, steel guitars from a third. With careful editing, the Blazer Music sounded terrific. With that music, we had our announcer do a voice-over, "This is Portland Trail Blazer basketball . . . "

"I told the woman that the Blazer Music wasn't available in stores," Sue said, "but she was persistent, almost panicking."

The woman told Sue why she desperately needed the Blazer Music that day. Her husband had died, and his final request was that when he was lowered into the ground, he wanted the Blazer Music to be played.

"I called the studio," Sue said, "and their chief engineer is on vacation. Our original music is locked up someplace there and nobody can get to it. The only thing I have is a tape of one of our broadcasts, which has all the billboards on it." (Billboards are the short sponsor identifications at the beginning of sports broadcasts.)

"Is that okay with the woman?" I asked.

"Yes," Sue said, "she's that desperate."

"Fine, give her a copy."

Sue delivered the tape, and we sent flowers.

The next day, this dead Blazer fan was lowered into the ground. At the graveside, the woman pushed the start button on the tape machine. There was a drum roll. Then there were exciting audio highlights from one of our games, "Thompson with the rebound, the outlet pass to Valentine, he's going lickety brindle down the middle, pass to Kenny Carr on the wing and he jammed it. Rip city!"

Then the music lowered and the announcer gave the billboards. The mourners at graveside heard—and maybe even our dead fan heard, "This is Portland Trail Blazer basketball . . . Blazer basketball is brought to you by Budweiser—know when to say no—and by Chevrolet—the heartbeat of America—and by Safeway . . . "

So, even at the end, we were pitching the benefits of our sponsors. . . .

■

"You know, if I sign this sponsorship proposal of yours," Al Neish, the advertising manager of Safeway in Oregon said, "I could get fired."

This was a long time ago, circa 1979, and Al's words have stuck with me like gum you step on in a parking lot during a hot summer day. Wherever I have worked, whether it be running a pro sports team or doing consulting, the echo of Al's words—*I could get fired*—were within hearing range. His words put a different perspective for me on selling. Without knowing it, Al's words put a critical spin on an early development of jump-start marketing.

IN-HOUSE OR THE OUTHOUSE?

I was shocked when Al said he could get fired by buying something I was selling. I was just trying to sell him something; I wasn't looking at this as a life-or-death job situation.

I had just started with the Portland Trail Blazers, and we had brought radio "in-house." Bringing radio in-house meant that the team took the financial risk of the radio broadcasts of its games. In the past, a radio station would offer a team money for the rights to broadcast the games. All the expenses were the responsibility of the station—the announcers, the phone lines (now satellite linkups), and what they paid the team. When we brought radio in-house, we hired the announcers, paid for their traveling expenses, and hired the sales and support people. In other words, the Blazers were then responsible for all of the expenses in putting that broadcast on the air. The radio station had no financial risk at all in airing the games. The game broadcasts became a no-risk, tune-in promotion for the station.

This shift of financial responsibility only worked for the Blazers if we sold more sponsorships than the radio station did. If we didn't, then the experiment of bringing radio in-house would send my career to the outhouse.

The Trail Blazers were generally credited as the first team to bring radio in-house. I don't think that we were, but I do know that we were the first to make it a major profit center. For instance, in the 1978–79 season, the Blazers were one of the elite teams in the NBA. Just two years before, Bill Walton led the team to the NBA championship. A Portland radio station paid the Blazers a fee of $50,000 for the rights to broadcast the games. In those days, that was about the third- or fourth-best rights-fee deal in the NBA. When we brought our radio broadcasts in-house, I repositioned and repackaged the sponsorships. With the repositioning and repackaging came new pricing, which delivered a net profit of $900,000! This was at a time when entire team payrolls were about $1.5 million. That jump in profit was a shot heard throughout the NBA.

As you would expect, the new pricing wasn't easily accepted by sponsors in Portland. Safeway had purchased a sponsorship the previous year for $19,000. I was proposing a sponsorship deal to Al for $130,000. After the initial meeting, where I think Al threatened to have me ground up as hamburger in the Safeway meat market, we sat down again. While the price increase was ludicrous and seemingly unconscionable, there was a lot more substance to the sponsorship than just radio commercials during the game.

Safeway's sponsorship package included radio commercials, but every radio station had those. Our differentiation was that we provided some unique promotions utilizing the celebrity status of the players and the team. These promotions would *increase* Safeway's business.

Al said to me, "I hate to say this, but your sponsorship with the promotions at $130,000 is a better sponsorship than the one that I bought at $19,000." That was not an easy admission for Al. In Portland, he was regarded as the toughest, shrewdest adman in the West. "But I've got a boss. He'd think I was an idiot for increasing our expenditure that much for the Blazers. I might be able to get this approved, but if your promotions don't work, I could get fired."

A week or so later, Al got the sponsorship approved from his boss. We now had a commitment from Safeway for $130,000, but we also had the responsibility of Al's career. Selling was no longer selling to me.

REVERSING THE WEIGHT OF RESPONSIBILITY

When a radio station sells a company some of its airtime to play the company's commercial, the station's commitment is pretty clear. The commitment by the radio station ends when the commercial runs. The only thing that the station has promised is to run the commercial. If the commercial is not persuasive, no problem. That is the responsibility of the company's ad agency. When we brought radio in-house and dramatically raised the rate, putting Al's career on the block, there was a massive shift of responsibility.

Our responsibility wasn't to just air the commercials. Our responsibility was to somehow, some way make Safeway's sponsorship *successful.* To do this, the promotions had to increase sales. In the process, we wanted to make Al a hero at Safeway.

MAKING THE CLIENT A HERO

Making the client a hero takes a whole different spin on selling. This different spin is an important jump-start element. Sure, it might seem easier to just train a sales staff in hand-to-hand combat to get new business. I think that hammer-and-tong sales techniques work in the short term. Generally, these techniques create an almost adversarial relationship between the salesperson and the customer. After the short term, this type of company would need to jump-start itself again just to replace the customers that were gained and then lost by the hammer-and-tong approach.

When a company takes on the philosophy of making the client a hero, then the principles of jump-start marketing produce results that can be staggering. New business is built on top of *renewing* business. Making a client a hero guarantees that you'll have a friend for another year. A company making all of its clients heroes guarantees that it will have lots of friends for another year. Now that's something that a company can really build on!

Once we developed this concept, it worked wonders for us in Portland. We would rarely lose a sponsor. We layered new heroes onto "renewing heroes." And sponsorship sales grew in geometric proportions:

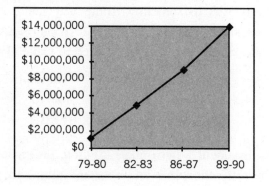

Blazer Sponsorship Growth

I took this concept of making the client a hero with me when I went to the New Jersey Nets. The concept was a major contributor to our sponsorship growth: *new* business being built on top of *renewing* business.

DOING A TERRIFIC JOB MAY NOT BE ENOUGH

Have you heard this before? "We bust our tails for our clients and they don't appreciate us."

Or how about this? "We did everything we said we would

do, but we don't get the renewal. Some company comes along and undercuts our price, and they get the business."

When I hear this, I usually ask a question. "Does the decision-maker at the client know this?" In some cases, the decision-maker is the purchasing agent. In other cases, it might be an executive of the company. In advertising, the decision-maker might not even be an employee of the client; it might be the client's advertising agency. In many of the cases, however, the decision-maker is *not* the person working on a day-to-day basis with your people.

The response to whether the decision-maker knows what a terrific job the company is doing is usually, "Well, uh . . . no."

Then I'll ask another question. "Who would tell the decision-maker what a terrific job you're doing?"

"I assume his people must be telling him."

"His people? What if 'his people' screw something up? Do they take the blame or do they shift the blame to you?"

"Blame us."

Once that sinks in, I'll ask two more questions.

I'll ask, "If the company isn't working with the decision-maker on a day-to-day basis, how are they going to make that person a hero?"

Instead of waiting for an answer, I'll ask, "Does the *boss* of the decision-maker know what a terrific decision the decision-maker made?"

It's not enough to just do a terrific job for a client.

HOW TO MAKE A CLIENT A HERO

Whenever we sold a sponsorship while I was at the New Jersey Nets, I felt that the decision-maker was sticking his or her neck out. The sponsor was taking a leap of faith that we would do what we said we would do. We couldn't allow that neck to stick out into a noose or a guillotine.

Buying a sponsorship with the Nets seemed to be a far riskier thing than what Al Neish had done when he bought a sponsorship with the Portland Trail Blazers. The decision-maker's neck would be stuck out due to the past decade's hapless performance of the Nets. The Nets' identity was *loser.* It would be far less riskier to buy a sponsorship with the New York Knicks or New York Giants or New York Yankees. Sticking your neck out for an established loser could indeed be risky.

There are naysayers in any company. Some of these naysayers want to climb ahead even if they cause someone else to fall. I'm sure that when the decision-maker of a company bought a sponsorship with the Nets that it caught the attention of the naysayers in the executive ranks. With the decision-maker's neck stuck out, a naysayer might even help tie the noose or grease up the guillotine.

So, as in the case with Al in Portland, we were going to make whoever bought a sponsorship with the Nets a hero.

There was one way to do it:

1. Prove it to the decision-maker's boss.

We weren't going to prove it to the decision-maker's boss by calling up on the phone and saying, "Joe did a great job in deciding to buy our product." We were first going to prove it to the decision-maker. With the proof that we provided, the decision-maker could use it as a tool to fend off any naysayers and prove to his boss what a great decision it was. Proving it to the decision-maker was a three-step process.

1: Do a terrific job. At the Portland Trail Blazers or the New Jersey Nets, we had a philosophy with sponsors that we lived by: *Do whatever it takes to make the sponsorship successful.*

Remember, we weren't like the radio station whose commitment was to run a company's commercial. That was the radio station's measure of success—playing the commercial. Our commitment was to make the sponsorship successful.

There are many different ways that a team can make a sponsorship successful. Whichever way it was, our mandate to ourselves was still always: *Do whatever it takes to make the sponsorship successful.* When a company has that mind-set, your people get very creative in making it work. They can't blame the client for failure; they can only blame themselves.

2: Provide an "annual report." A lot of elements go into a sponsorship of a pro sports team. The decision-maker wouldn't, of course, experience all of those elements. In many cases, the decision-maker would see just a few of the elements. Our annual report covered all of the elements for that particular sponsorship and how the sponsor benefited.

Inside the annual report were the following sections:

Executive summary. This was in the form of a cover letter. The letter outlined the tangible benefits of the sponsorship. Along with my signature and title, everyone who worked on the sponsorship signed the letter. In some cases, this would mean that nine or ten people would sign the letter.

Summary points of each element of the sponsorship. Each element of the sponsorship was clearly defined as to the purpose and value to the sponsor.

Promotional support details. When a sponsor had a consumer promotion, we told the sponsor that we would take care of all the details involved in promoting it to our fans. We had a lot of weapons on hand. For instance, we could have our announcers talk about the special promotion on radio and TV games. We would feature the promotion in a mailing to our ticket holders. We would advertise the promotion in the newspaper. In this section, we detailed each promotional step we took and the value of those steps.

Samples of each element of the sponsorship. Each major sponsor received items that included season tickets, advertising on the backs of tickets for at least one game, a full-page ad in our media guide, etc. In this section, we featured one item per page with a brief description of that item.

In some cases, the annual report was an inch-thick full documentation of the sponsorship. It had colorful samples, there was no phony hype on its pages, and it was professionally bound. On the spine of the report was the sponsor's name and team's name, such as Safeway's *Sponsorship of the Portland Trail Blazers, 1984–85.*

This book was designed to be displayed by the client. It could be a "coffee table"-type book that was placed in an executive seating area in the client's personal office. Or it could easily sit on the client's credenza.

3: Hyping the client. If I sent you one of our sponsorship annual reports, you would be able to:

A. Easily read through it.
B. Understand the key components of the sponsorship.

C. Come to the conclusion that the company benefited from the sponsorship.
D. Realize that whoever bought the sponsorship was a bright and shrewd person.
E. See that the decision-maker should be given a raise.
F. See that the decision-maker should be promoted.

That was the real purpose of the annual report: *to help make the client look good because of our sponsorship.* We wanted to make the client the hero.

We gave each client at least four copies of their annual report. If the client wanted more, we provided more. We could assume that one copy made it to the client's *boss.* We knew that a second copy would make it to the client's boss, because we sent one to the boss with a short note from me.

HOW YOUR OWN STAFF BENEFITS FROM AN ANNUAL REPORT

When we started to do the annual reports, our staff started to get better. *Much better.* I was stunned at our extreme attention to even the smallest detail in executing each sponsorship. That was great! As we know, there is always a devilish small detail that can drive you crazy. My rule of thumb on small details is:

The small detail that is overlooked eventually becomes the most important detail.

We no longer had those small details jump up and become monsters. And even when one of the small details did somehow evade scrutiny, we were far better equipped to quickly

the problem before the small detail started to take on a
f its own. I attribute much of the improvement of our
execution to our annual reports.

You can probably picture it: a staff putting together an annual report that's purpose is to make the client a hero. The staff is poring over the details. "Uh-oh," one staff member says, "we really didn't do a very good job on this portion. This won't make anybody a hero. In fact, it could make somebody a goat—including us."

To protect against the "goat" status, staffers started to anticipate what could go wrong. That might sound like pessimistic thinking, but it was great mental preparation in executing the sponsorships. Many of the little details that could spring up and bite you were anticipated and solved before they could come to life.

WHY DON'T MORE COMPANIES DO ANNUAL REPORTS FOR CLIENTS?

You would think that making the client a hero by providing something like an annual report takes a lot of work. It does. But as we learned in the second year, not as much work as you might think.

The first year we prepared annual reports for our major sponsors, there were plenty of late nights at the office. You see, at the end of the basketball season, we tried to re-create history. We had to gather all the details of the past six months and rethink all the great things that we had done in executing the sponsorship. It took us *hours* putting together just one sponsorship annual report.

The second year, we got smarter. We started preparing the

annual reports from the beginning of the season. When we ran a newspaper ad to promote a sponsor's consumer promotion, we clipped the ad and put it in the sponsor's file. When we ran radio spots to promote a sponsor's consumer promotion, we transferred the media schedule into the sponsor's file on our computers. So each time there was an activity with a sponsor, it was filed. At the end of the season, we collated all the information and, *voilà*, we had a dazzling sponsorship annual report done in about an hour!

Sure, we had to spend seconds and minutes throughout the season compiling our annual report. Those seconds and minutes weren't as intimidating as the prospect of hours if we waited until the end of the season to prepare the sponsorship annual report.

Are those seconds and minutes worth it? Let's look at the two great benefits in making the client a hero:

1: **You have your client for a friend (and customer) for at least another year.** If you make a client a hero, how vulnerable are you to your competition stealing the business? You're not vulnerable, you're bulletproof! Would any client give you up? Of course not.

2: **Your staff becomes far more efficient at execution.** When the staff is involved in trying to make the client a hero, they make themselves heroes by far superior execution.

It's a small price that will deliver those two benefits. *Seconds and minutes.* Just think, seconds and minutes to hand-deliver supreme client loyalty and a more efficient staff.

Not a bad price at all.

A Simple Test You Can Take

(Multiple choice.) **What's the most important step in making the client a hero?**

    A. Send the client on a junket to Las Vegas.
    B. Do what you say you're going to do.
    C. Prove it to the client's boss that he or she is a hero.

What is the three-step process in proving it to the client's boss?

    A. First step: _____
    B. Second step: _____
    C. Third step: _____

How can you take the concept of the annual report and apply it to your business?

_____

_____

Making the client a hero wouldn't work for which businesses?

_____

_____

Answers

1. You might have answered (B). Well, that answer is wrong. I'm assuming that you would do what you said you would do. But

just doing what you said you would do doesn't make your client a hero. I've seen companies do more than what they said they would do and still lose the business. If you take the extra step in making your client a hero, you've got a friend (and client) for at least another year. So the answer to this question is (C).

A. *First step:* Do a terrific job.

B. *Second step:* Provide an annual report. The annual report will vary from industry to industry. Remember, this is a tool that helps underscore how wonderful you are by documenting what a terrific job you did.

C. *Third step:* Hyping the client. This is using your version of the annual report to make the client look like a hero. Make sure that this gets into the hands of your client's boss.

2. Around the time that we were developing the annual report idea, a friend of mine had stopped by my house one night. While I was on the phone, he picked up this thick book that was sitting on our kitchen table. It was the annual report of a client. He leafed through it.

When I got off the phone, my friend said, "Geez, this company got a helluva deal from you guys." He was clearly impressed.

I nodded and then told him about our philosophy of making the client a hero.

"Well, you sure did that," he said. "I think he's a hero and I don't even know him."

A moment later, he asked, "I wonder how I could make this work in my business?" (He was in the real estate business.) "I don't need my customer to be a friend for another year," he said. "I have sold them a house and the chances are that I won't sell them another. If I did sell them another, it wouldn't be for another seven or eight years. And besides, when I sell a couple a house, they are their own bosses."

"Make them a hero to themselves then," I said. "Who knows, you may get a lot of referrals."

My friend fiddled around with the idea for a couple of months and came up with a format. It wasn't as elaborate as our sponsorship annual report, but if you have ever bought a house, what would you think about getting his report?

It was four pages. On the cover was a four-color picture of the house that was purchased. On the inside cover, my friend had the heading "The Search."

Under this heading, he had listed each house that they had visited in looking for the house that they wanted to buy and call home. He had clipped the little pictures from the multiple-listing book and pasted them next to the day and date that they had looked at the house. If they had looked at a lot of houses, he just clipped the few houses that they were most interested in and had a listing of the rest.

The next page had the heading "The Choice." In this section, he had the multiple-listing picture and listing information. In a written narrative, my friend wrote why the people had liked the house.

On the back page was a section titled "The Negotiations." He summarized the offers and counteroffers with day, date, etc.

On the same page was the heading "The Financing." Here he had all the pertinent information of who the lending institution was, the name of the person they dealt with, the interest rate, etc. At the bottom of the page was a picture of my friend and the couple that he had taken at the closing. He listed his name, address, phone, and fax numbers. This was a terrific summary of the largest purchase that a couple would normally make.

"I've done this four times," my friend said. "People are sort of stunned when I give them this. I have made them heroes. And I guess I've done all right in their eyes, too."

A couple of months later, my friend said that his annual reports were driving him crazy. I asked why.

"For every report that I do, I get at least two unsolicited referrals," my friend said. "People love to show my report to friends. When they're thinking about buying a house—and selling their own in the process—I get the call. What is amazing about this is that everybody knows a real estate agent. But I'm getting the calls because of that annual report idea."

"So what's wrong with that?" I asked.

"Well, I'm working all the time and my golf game has gone into the sewer. It's so bad, you're going to have to give me two strokes per side. . . . "

3. Retailers who have small dollar transactions. If you're selling a $10 item, it's doubtful that you could make the buyer a hero. However, if you're selling a $35,000 car, you certainly could make the buyer a hero. One way would be to follow the format of my real estate friend.

The headings would be different, of course, but the concept could work just as well.

14. THE SECRET WEAPON

Ground rule #14: Run interference for your budding superstars.

"Can you drop whatever plans you have and have lunch with me today?" a friend asked over the phone.

The only plan I had was that I was going to have a quick soup and sandwich at a nearby deli. My friend sounded desperate. I thought perhaps that he was a victim of downsizing. Wrong. He was going to do the downsizing. He was going to fire an employee.

Over lunch he said, "This is really tough. This is really hard on me."

I wasn't very sympathetic. "Don't give me that crap," I said. "You still have a job. The person that you're firing doesn't."

I could speak from experience. I had been on both sides of the fence. I have fired people. I have been fired. Believe me, it's not fun firing people. But it's far less fun to get fired.

When my friend started into a monologue about the whole situation, my mind drifted. I was thinking about the time I was fired by the Denver Nuggets. I thought about how awful I felt, how betrayed I felt. There's no way that the guy that fired me could have felt that bad. But as I brought back my thoughts of the day I was fired, a smile crossed my face.

"What the hell is so funny?" my friend asked. "Here I am just bleeding all over and you're smiling."

"I was just thinking about the time I was fired."

"I didn't know you were fired," he said. "Hell, even though you're working for the Nets, your career has turned out all right. You're smiling—you're on the verge of a big laugh, so tell me about you being fired. It might make me feel better."

So here's my story about being fired.

Eight months before I took the job with the Nuggets, I quit the Portland Trail Blazers. When I resigned from the Blazers, a lot of people thought I was crazy for quitting. After all, I was one of the highest paid executives in the NBA, I was living in the Great Northwest, we had been doing highly innovative things at the Blazers, and we were a model pro franchise. Why quit, for God's sake?

I simply felt it was time to move on. Paul Allen, the cofounder of Microsoft, bought the team from Larry Weinberg. Larry was a terrific pro team owner. Besides caring tremendously about the people, the fans, and the community, Larry encouraged me to try new stuff, to do breakthrough things. It was a fun and exhilarating eleven years working for Larry. In fact, if Larry ever bought another team, I'd work for him for free.

After Paul bought the team, I saw that things were going to change. They weren't necessarily going to change for the worse— or the better—they were just going to change. The corporate culture that we had installed would be different, and I didn't want to be a part of that change.

Since I had a small share of the team when it was sold, I felt financially secure. I even had a clause in my contract that if the club was sold, I could leave at any time and be paid the balance of the contract. That balance carried me for eight months.

My wife and I traveled. I played a lot of golf. I started a summer basketball league for college players. It was fun. And then, on my seventh month away from the Blazers, David Stern, the commissioner of the NBA, called.

He told me that two African-Americans were buying the Denver Nuggets. He had arranged the financing. He said that he really wanted to see this breakthrough minority ownership work, and would I consult with the Nuggets?

Two weeks later, I wasn't consulting. I was named president and general manager of the Nuggets. My first day on the job was opening day of the season. Starting when the season started preempted a lot of the things I could do in marketing. You see, most of team marketing is done in the off-season.

I was president and general manager for ninety days. During that time, I thought I did some of my best marketing. On the ninety-first day, I was fired. Peter Bynoe, the managing partner, came into my office with the team's attorney. "Things aren't working out," he said.

"What do you mean?" I asked.

"Things aren't working out. We want to make a change." It seems that they needed to "shoot the messenger" to appease a large investor. You see, in my first month on the job, I locked our accountants into a room with me for about a week. I wanted to do a "realistic" cash flow and not rely on the one that had been presented by the previous owner. The previous cash flow showed that they would need no extra cash to run the team. Even with more aggressive projections on revenue, my cash flow showed that an additional $1.5 million would be needed in the next eighteen months. After that time, we would consistently make a profit.

After the accountants and I had created the new cash flow charts, I called a meeting with the owners. I knew they would be shocked, but I hoped they wouldn't be dangerous.

I started the meeting by saying, "The cash flow that was used to purchase the team was fiction. We've come up with a nonfiction version. However, I hope this won't be the case of shooting the messenger . . . "

The messenger was indeed shot. It was a jolt to me. I hadn't seen it coming. I hadn't even seen the bullet being put in the gun.

"I know you have a five-year contract, and we're going to honor it," Peter said.

It was a very lucrative contract. However, it had an "offset" clause, where if I took another job, they could deduct what I made from the other job from what they paid me over the five years.

I thought it would be cleaner and better to waive the five-year deal and make an on-the-spot, one-lump-sum cash settlement.

"Let's settle it right now," I said. Then I asked if I could call my lawyer. Peter nodded.

I called my Portland attorney, Owen Blank.

After saying hello, I said to Owen, "I've been fired and I'd like to come up with a contract settlement right now. I'm going to put you on the speaker phone."

For about twenty minutes, we negotiated. It came down to four clauses. One of the clauses listed the cash settlement. I typed it up on my computer and printed out two copies. Peter and I signed both copies and we kept one each.

Peter had called a press conference, and he wanted me to appear. I did. He told the press that I was resigning for personal reasons. I guess the personal reasons were that they didn't want me around. When a reporter asked me if I wanted to elaborate on the personal reasons, I said, "No." That was the only word I spoke at the press conference. There was no mention about the messenger being shot.

I went back to Portland, Oregon.

My wife and I traveled, again. I played a lot of golf, again. And we took a lot of day trips to the Oregon coast—about an hour-and-a-half drive. We really enjoyed the tremendous beauty of Oregon. Eventually, we bought a house right on the beachfront.

We noticed that other people on the Oregon coast named their beach houses things like "The Road's End" or "Our Paradise." They would have little wood plaques with the names of their beach houses nailed to the street-side walls.

We named our beach house, although we never went through the formality of a wood plaque. We just call it "The Nugget House."

Even with "The Nugget House" to salve my wounds, I can't rank being fired as one of my top-ten life experiences. That's why I didn't give much sympathy to my friend.

I asked my friend whether the person who was to be fired was under contract. Maybe there was a "Nugget House" in it for him to soften the blow. No such luck, no contract.

I asked about termination pay. My friend said that their company didn't provide much.

"Bargain for more termination pay," I told my friend. "Yes, sometimes changes have to be made. But you're looking to make a change, not screw the person. There's three good reasons for giving the person more termination pay."

My friend sat still, listening.

"The first reason is for the person that is being fired. Give that person a fair chance to go out in the marketplace and get a job. After all, this person is an executive, not a cook at McDonald's. It sometimes takes awhile to get back on track. The person that you described isn't a bad person, it's just somebody that has a different philosophy than you. Don't make it a crime. Just make the change, don't screw the guy.

"The second reason is for yourself. Look how you got all worked up. Well, *you're* going to feel better, because you're not screwing the guy. You'll sleep well tonight.

"The third reason could be the most important one," I said. "This one is for the rest of the employees. Firings are tough on everybody. But most of your employees figure that this guy has to go. They won't be shocked. What they will appreciate is that you just didn't get him in the car, drive ninety-miles-an-hour down the freeway, and then push him out the door. Your employees will see and appreciate that if you're fair to the people that you fire, you'll really be fair to those that aren't fired.

"These people are essential to your success. They are your secret weapon."

■

I've never been involved with a team that won a world championship. I can only imagine that the feeling is absolutely terrific. It's got to be even more than the shared glory that the fans feel.

Imagine how the Houston Rockets employees felt when their team won their first NBA championship in 1994. Whatever elation they felt, however, was short-lived. Two weeks after Hakeem Olajuwon led the Rockets to the championship, the Houston Rockets fired over 75 percent of their front-office employees.

This wasn't a downsizing strategy. Rocket management just felt that they needed new front-office people. A *lot* of new front-office people.

While it wasn't as dramatic, the Portland Trail Blazers lost more than 50 percent of their staff. This wasn't a line-them-up-against-the-wall mass firing like the Rockets. This took a couple of years, between 1994 and 1996. More than sixty employees left the Blazers and their team-owned arena. They were either fired or they left on their own. One employee told me that he left before "the Blazers found a bullet with his name on it."

These examples aren't the norm, nor is it the norm for the "outside world." But mass forced exodus of employees does exist. When I see an organization with a regular high turnover, I think like a marketing person. I ask myself one question:

How in the world are these types
of organizations supposed to make
the client a hero when the staffs spend
much of their time ducking bullets?

THE BEATINGS WILL STOP WHEN THE MORALE IMPROVES

When there is high turnover, you can bet that one of the priorities of the company is *not* making the client a hero. Heck, the priority is staying employed, not making the client a hero! It's "Look, I'll get in the lifeboat first, then I'll help you in (heh, heh, heh)."

If you like the concept of the previous chapter and want to make your client a hero—and you should, because it is a terrific way to build a business—then there are two steps you have to take to get into that position. You don't have to be the president of your company to initiate these steps. You could be a department head.

If you don't have anyone reporting to you and there is high turnover, then there is just one step for you to take. Stay late one day, photocopy your résumé, and turn yourself over to another company.

For those who have people reporting to them, here are the two steps to take to stop the turnover of at least your own people:

1: **Place your time and emphasis with your budding superstars; leave the poor attitude people alone or fire them.** Most managers in business often think like a head coach in the NBA. An NBA head coach will always have some talented players who are either poorly motivated or have a sloppy work ethic. The coach will spend an inordinate amount of time trying to motivate these players or improve their work habits.

These coaches will stay up nights trying to solve these types of puzzles. They should have slept instead. I've seen some of the best coaches and managers in business chew up their guts over how to motivate a poorly motivated person. The poorly motivated person doesn't even care. The best way to motivate a poorly motivated player is to not try. It's better to spend the time and the energy with your budding superstars. These people already want to improve. With a little help and attention, they'll grow in geometric progression.

Stay up nights and think how you can bring a budding superstar along faster. Perks and favors? Yeah, they should go to the budding superstars.

Isn't this favoritism? Sure it is. You're favoring the people who are making your department or company and you better.

Shouldn't everybody be treated equally? Of course not. In many cases, the poorly motivated worker (or player) receives more attention than the budding superstar. That doesn't make any sense at all.

By placing your time and energy on your budding superstars, you're less likely to lose them to another company. After all, they are learning, they are improving, and they've got a boss who showers them with positive attention.

With this type of attention to budding superstars, what type of message are you sending to new employees in your department? The new employees will see the clear upside of working hard. They will then make a choice. Most people would choose to put in a little better effort and join the favored team.

Does this mean that you should be a tyrant to the poorly motivated worker? No, not at all. Just accept that person for what he or she is. Don't take negative steps in the way you treat that person, but don't exert energy in thinking that you can "save" that person either. Use that energy to boost your budding superstars.

2: Create systems and procedures that allow your budding superstars to succeed. Years ago, a newspaper writer was doing a story on the Portland Trail Blazer organization, and he asked me, "You must be a great motivator. Everybody here seems to be so enthusiastic and energetic."

I listened and nodded. "I've got two secrets," I said.

The writer clicked his ballpoint pen and poised it over his pad of paper.

I paused. I was going to play this for maximum effect.

"The first secret is that I only hire self-motivated people," I said. I paused while he wrote.

"The second secret is I try not to do things that would unmotivate them."

I thought I was pretty good at that—at not doing things that would unmotivate a self-motivated person. I really learned that while consulting with other teams and companies *after* I left the Blazers.

When you come in to consult with a team, the first thing that smacks you in the face is that the team in trouble doesn't have systems that allow people to be successful. That's right— systems that would *not* allow the workers to reach maximum levels of success.

How could that ever be? After all, the bosses *want* to be successful, right? In many cases, their income is tied to the success of the company.

If you went on a nationwide search, I don't think you would find one boss who did not want to succeed. Knowing that *all* bosses want to succeed, why do they somehow set up roadblocks that actually limit their people's ability to succeed?

It might be the ivory tower complex.

It might be the perks that distort their thinking.

It might be the seniority.

It could be all of the above causing them to be afraid of trying new things that would remove the roadblocks. Thus, companies that are unsuccessful usually have faulty systems with a lot of rules and regulations that keep the employees on that faulty path. Employees that try to jump off that path either leave or they are fired or ostracized.

If you're the president of a company, a department head, or just the leader of a terrorist marketing group, there are things to look for in faulty systems. When you find these things, it then becomes simple. In your area of influence, change those things that need to be changed.

There are two areas that can create systems that don't allow people to be successful. These two areas are cherished by the lesser motivated employee and despised by the budding superstars.

We've always done it that way. This is the first tip that something is wrong.

During my ninety days with the Denver Nuggets, I asked a lot of questions. One of them was about our day-of-game advertising that was used to attract the walk-up ticket buyers. "We spend $5,000 a game in newspaper advertising and radio spots. Why?"

"We've always done it that way," was the consistent response from several people. *RED ALERT!*

The walk-up buyers contributed only $8,000 to the gate receipts. We were spending $5,000 to get $8,000.

I asked, "What if we didn't spend the $5,000 in day-of-game advertising? Would we still get the $8,000 per game in walk-up business?"

"Probably."

We discontinued the day-of-game advertising. The walk-up gate receipts stayed at about $8,000. If the people would have given a better answer than "we've always done it that way," I might have just nodded my head and gone onto another subject. However, "we've always done it that way" is almost always a red alert that something needs to be changed.

For each red alert that is allowed to remain in place, you've got a potential hurdle that will slow down the growth of your budding superstars. These hurdles don't bother your lesser motivated people. They feel comfortable and secure with these red alerts. The lesser motivated people will show emotion when you try to change the way it's always been done.

So you have a choice:

- Keep the way things have always been done. Your lesser motivated people will feel comfortable and secure, and your budding superstars will get frustrated and look to jump ship.

- Start improving the way things have always been done. Your budding superstars will notice; they'll feel that they have a chance to grow big-time. Your lesser motivated people will shrug their shoulders, sigh, and continue on.

I've got a secret. For companies that have a high turnover, it seems that their employees have been trained by the CIA. Everything seems to be a secret. I'm not referring to a secret formula like Coca-Cola's, I'm referring to everyday stuff. This is an abusive use of the power of secrecy.

As a consultant, I've seen some amazing acts of stupid secrecy:

- *Sponsorship sales secrets.* Many teams will not tell their salespeople what sponsorships have been sold and for how much. I asked a VP-sponsorships of a team why. "We don't want the competition to find out who our sponsors are and how much each spends."

  That sounded like CIA training.

  "But your own salespeople don't know exactly what has been sold and what is available," I said.

  "Sure they do," the VP-sponsorships said. "I verbally tell them about inventory that is available on a need-to-know basis."

  Need-to-know. It seems like the sponsorship salespeople should know what has been sold and for how much and what is left to sell.

  At one time, I had wondered what had happened to all the spies after the Cold War ended. Now I knew. Many of them had ended up in team sports.

- *Budget secrets.* When I started consulting with the New Jersey Nets, only two people knew what the budget was: the chairman and the chief financial officer. Department heads weren't on a need-to-know basis even concerning the budgets of their own departments. Every expenditure had to be approved either by the chairman or the CFO. The rule of thumb was not to spend on anything. In other words, *save your way to oblivion.*

While the above may seem extreme, variations of the above abound in every company. Why? Has the end of the Cold War unleashed that many spies into business?

Of course, there is a simple solution.

Declassify everything. Well, almost everything. You wouldn't declassify any secret formulas. You wouldn't declassify salaries. Declassify everything else.

Will some of this declassified information end up with your competitors? Maybe.

Will some of your people resent losing this power base of secrecy? Probably.

However, by declassifying almost everything, you're removing hurdles that will slow down your budding superstars. You're allowing them to see some of the bigger picture. You're allowing them to grow. You're allowing yourself to grow. You're allowing your department or company to grow.

THE MORALE WILL IMPROVE WHEN JUMP-START MARKETING IS USED

It's easy to spot the culprit in a company with high turnover. Just look at the top. I've never seen high turnover caused by the janitor.

For whatever reason, that top person is running that company for the moment. The company is living for short-term growth. Let the future be damned. Because of the movement of people, it may seem that there is more opportunity, but the real opportunity is when that top person is replaced and, to make up for past guillotine tactics, the company has to resort to jump-start marketing.

A Simple Test You Can Take

(Fill in the blanks.) **What are the two steps to take to reduce turnover of key employees?**

    A. _____

    B. _____

(Fill in the blanks.) **What are the two things to look for that create faulty systems that don't allow employees to succeed to their fullest potential?**

    A. _____

    B. _____

(Fill in the blanks.) **In your organization, which things that have "always been done that way" need to be changed now?**

Item   Should change by

_____

_____

Answers

1. A. Place your time and emphasis with your budding superstars; leave the poor attitude people alone or fire them.

    B. Create systems and procedures that allow your budding superstars to succeed.

These answers might anger the lesser motivated employees. These employees believe in seniority more than in being fully productive. Because they have senior status, and most likely higher pay, these people are least likely to leave. The people that will leave are the younger, budding superstars. Those are the people that you can't afford to have leave.

By creating a system that allows your budding superstars to succeed, the lesser motivated employees will eventually be outnumbered. They will either join in or opt out. Either way, your company wins. Major turnover has been avoided and you're able to make your client the hero on a regular basis.

We've always done it that way. A companion to this is: If it ain't broke, don't fix it. On the surface, this *sounds* logical. In reality, if you don't try to *improve* something that isn't broke, you'll walk in one morning and find it in shambles. Things change—everything changes—and improving something that is not broken has to be a regular part of a corporate lifestyle.

I've got a secret. This is false power. If it is rampant in an organization, it will drive the budding superstars away. Then you're left with the lesser motivated senior employees.

"I've Got a Secret" was a long-running TV show in the 1950s and 1960s. However, to keep your budding superstars, it's time to close out that show. Declassify!

2. I might not have provided you with enough paper for this. So bring out your yellow legal pad and start writing down things that have "always been done that way." Don't worry about priorities. Just write.

There are things that will fall into your list that don't exactly fit the "always done that way" criteria. Don't worry about that, just write it down.

I'll give you an example of one of those things that don't quite fit "always been done that way." Early in my ninety-day tenure with the Denver Nuggets, I went to the box office before the game. I knocked on the door and somebody from the inside yelled, "Who is it?"

I yelled back my name through the door.

I heard the locks being undone, and the door swung open. The box office manager furtively looked out down one hallway, then the other, and motioned me inside. Inside there were four people selling tickets to fans who had decided to come to the game. I hung around for about half an hour, talking to the people between sales.

The next day, the box office manager came to my office. He said, "That's the first time that an executive of the Nuggets has ever been in the box office."

I laughed. I said, "That's the most important office we have. That's where the money comes in."

"That's what I came to talk to you about," the box office manager said. "It's about a peephole."

"What do you mean?"

"When you came up, you knocked on the door," he said. "We couldn't see you, so I had to yell out. You had to yell in to identify yourself. That was okay. But if one of us has to go to the restroom, we have to just step out. We've got a lot of cash in there, and once that door opens, somebody could be waiting and rush in and stick us up. We need a peephole."

"So get one," I said.

"For eight years, I've requisitioned for one, but it never gets anyplace. The arena is owned by the city, but we make the request through the Nuggets. The city and the Nuggets are always negotiating and renegotiating, and it seems a peephole never comes up."

"So what? Do you know somebody that could make a peephole?"

"Yes," he said.

"Could he get it done before tonight's game?" I asked.

"Sure."

"How much will it cost, do you think?" I asked.

"Seventy-five dollars or so."

"So let's do it. You're now the CEO of the peephole. Get it done." Off the box office manager went.

Just before tip-off, the box office manager tracked me down. I was giving an interview on TV. The box office manager waited. A few minutes later, I was finished. The box office manager said, "Come with me."

I followed him up to the box office. We stopped at the door. Imbedded in the door was a beautiful glass peephole. The box office manager was smiling.

For eight years, the lack of a peephole was bothering the box office manager and his staff. They felt management didn't care about their safety. The door to the box office had always been that way—without a peephole. With a drill and a little piece of glass, we changed all of that.

So, keep writing down "always been done that way" things. Even seemingly mundane things like doors that need peepholes. Once you've finished the list, start to number them in priority.

Prioritize two ways. Start numbering the most important "always been done that way" things that need to be changed. Then start numbering the "always been done that way" things that would be the easiest to change quickly.

Now start working your way down both lists. Start changing the "always been done that way" right now, including any doors that need peepholes.

15. AN OFFER THEY CAN'T REFUSE

Ground rule #15: Make it too good of a deal on purpose.

Everyone in sports knows that the toughest media market is New York City. The New York sports writers make Mike Wallace of "60 Minutes" seem like a pansy.

Part of the reason is the competition. When I was president of the New Jersey Nets, the New York City area had six daily newspapers. Each reporter was trying to scoop the field. A scoop didn't have to be something noteworthy, like a trade or the signing of a free agent. A scoop could be that one of our off-the-wall players, Chris Morris, wouldn't tie his shoelaces during practice.

When that "scoop" ran, it wasn't difficult for us to imagine the sports editor at each one of the other five daily newspapers jumping on their own beat writer. "How come you didn't get that story? You going soft on those bums? Follow up that didn't-tie-the-shoelaces story. Get the reactions of the owners, the GM, even that Spoelstra guy." Off and running the writers would go, and the Chris Morris didn't-tie-his-shoelaces story would develop a life of its own for about three days. This would gravitate over to the radio sports talk shows, and the fans would get their full say as to why Morris didn't tie his shoelaces.

As you can imagine, our cast of characters at the Nets provided endless stories. Very little of it was about the games that were played. It was the locker room scuffles or the AWOL players or the comic demands to be traded. Our guys practically hand-delivered these stories to the writers. It was almost *too* easy for the writers.

Somewhere along the line, I figured out a way that we could reverse the situation. We would only get positive stories written about the New Jersey Nets. This method wouldn't involve anything illegal or unethical. It wouldn't even involve trading our motley crew. It would just be a very unconventional way to automatically get good positive press all year long.

The idea was planted while I was having a cup of coffee in the media room before a Nets home game. Two of the writers were speculating that our coach, Butch Beard, was going to be fired at the end of the season. They were already speculating about Butch's successor.

I get tired and irritated about this type of useless speculation, so in frustration I asked, "What if we let you guys make the decision whether to keep Butch or not? If you choose to fire him, then you guys would select the head coach?"

"Ha," one writer said, "we'd do a better job of it."

"You might," I said. "So let's do it."

They both looked at me strangely.

"Both of you. You both get a ballot. And to make it fair, we'd also have to give the four other major newspapers a ballot."

They thought I was kidding, but I'm the same guy who sent rubber chickens to our season ticket holders (see next chapter's anecdote).

"There would be a few conditions that you would have to agree to," I said.

"Like what . . . ?"

"First of all, this would have to be our secret," I said. They nodded approval.

"The second condition is, if you vote to fire Butch, whoever gets the most votes to replace him has to be offered the job. No exceptions."

"What if Dan Quayle gets two votes and nobody else gets more than one?" one of the writers asked.

"I would think that you guys would be more responsible than that, but if Quayle was the choice, then we would have to go to Indiana and make Quayle the offer to be the head coach of the New Jersey Nets. Whoever the choice becomes, we have to go with it unanimously. Otherwise, we'd be arguing and wanting a revote, and then we'd be just like the owners that you guys rip in the paper all the time."

That made sense to the two writers.

"Yeah, we'd have to support the choice," the more cynical of the two writers said.

I imagined the headlines and excerpts from the stories from the six newspapers:

NETS NAME DAN QUAYLE HEAD COACH

"Brilliant choice."

"Will be a better coach than Pat Riley and Red Auerbach."

"Bold move will bring championship banners to the Meadowlands."

The more cynical writer asked, "What if one of these other guys breaks down and writes a negative story about the selection?" You knew that he was positioning himself to be the first writer to break ranks.

"That's the third condition," I said.

"We can't stop you, of course, from writing negative articles about the choice," I said. "After all, in America it's a free press. But if you do rip the new coach, then you lose your ballot for the next vote."

"What's the next vote?" the writer asked.

"Our decision on who to draft. Or which free agent we should sign. Or which trades we should make."

"That means we couldn't rip Yinka Dare," the other, a little less cynical writer, said. Yinka was our top draft choice in 1994. He went on to play three minutes his rookie year. His only shot was an air ball. The next season, he set an all-time NBA record—in 626 minutes of playing time, Yinka didn't get even one assist. That's the same amount of assists that a dead man would get if you laid him out on the playing floor for 626 minutes.

"But it would be worth it," the more cynical writer said. "We'd be building a championship."

While this is an absolutely crazy idea, there is a lot of common sense hidden inside the craziness. Beat writers are knowledgeable people who see every game. They're in the locker rooms, they're at courtside, they see a lot of things before a general manager does.

Like a general manager, these writers are frustrated. The general manager is frustrated because of the extreme scrutiny by the media about the moves that didn't work perfectly. The writers are frustrated because of the dumb moves they feel the general manager or owners have made. They feel they could have done better. A lot better.

Would the writers' decision be worse than the general manager's and owners'? Probably not. In fact, if you read the papers, each move would be bold, stunning, a stroke of genius, innovative, absolutely brilliant.

■

"This is too good of a deal," the director of operations said.

"What do you mean? Is it not profitable?" I asked.

"Sure, it's profitable, but it's too good of a deal for our fans," he said.

I was astounded. I was doing some consulting for the Hawaii Winter Baseball League. This is a player development league. The major leagues would send their best and brightest young stars to develop their baseball skills for two months in Hawaii. Japan and Korea sent their best young players, too. The players graduating from this league were the future superstars of the major baseball leagues from around the world. These young phenoms were divided up into four teams. They played games every day in October, November, and part of December.

While the brand of baseball was terrific and exciting, there was one problem. Nobody went to the games. Attendance was awful. Borrowing from the phrase in *Field of Dreams*, they built a league and nobody came. When nobody came, large pools of red ink formed in the offices of the league.

Enter Jon Spoelstra, the consultant.

One of the teams was located in Honolulu. We put a small sales staff together to sell more season tickets. In a couple of months, we had an over 100 percent increase in season ticket sales. That would have been great progress if the base had been 1,000 season tickets. Unfortunately, it was 100. So after a couple of months, we had sold only 200 season tickets. That would have erased just one small drop of red ink. But if you listen, customers will tell you what they want to buy.

From listening, we came up with some new ticket products. One was a picnic. If you've ever been to Hawaii on a weekend, you've noticed that Hawaiians love to picnic. With our picnic, you'd get a ticket for a game on a Saturday, all you could eat and drink, and a Honolulu Sharks baseball cap for $25.

All you can eat and drink for twenty-five bucks? The food was barbecue chicken and ribs, hot dogs, hamburgers, corn on the cob, beans, and salad. The drinks were soda and beer.

The profit on this was pretty good. The food service charged Hawaii Winter Baseball just $7 per person. The baseball cap cost $1.73. So out-of-pocket expenses were under $9 per person; profit was over $16 per person.

We were selling these picnics like crazy. One young salesperson sold $4,000 worth in one day. Another sold $2,000. Now we were making headway in mopping up that red ink!

"But it's *too good* of a deal," the director of operations said again. "Let's cut back on some things. Like the cap."

While I found this astounding, I shouldn't have. I had regularly seen this before. It's not unusual inside or outside of sports. Companies that are in need of a jump-start usually say that a new product idea is "too good of a deal."

MAKING IT TOO GOOD OF A DEAL ON PURPOSE

If you were given the assignment to make one of your products too good to refuse to buy, you'd have three paths to choose from:

1: **Keep lowering the price.** This is the most common way of making a product too good to refuse to buy. Drop the price 10 percent and see what happens. If the buyers don't buy, drop it another 10 to 20 percent, or even 50 percent. Keep on dropping the price and eventually it will be a product too good to refuse to buy. Maybe.

For this method to work, the value of the product has to be perceived as good at the original price. For instance, going to a Hawaii Winter Baseball game is one of the cheapest things you can do in Honolulu. The ticket costs just $6. And still, no one was buying at that price. Lowering the price by a dollar or even three wouldn't make that much difference.

The Whopper at Burger King has a perceived value that matches its $1.79 price. When it is discounted to 99¢, consumers jump and there is a surge in sales on the Whopper.

When there have been tens of thousands of cars sold at $20,000 each, a $3,000 factory rebate can produce a big spike in sales. Consumers perceived the value of the product at $20,000. Getting it for only $17,000 would be just cause to cut open the mattress and extract those thousands of dollars that have been stuffed in there.

Unless the product has a perceived value that equals the current price, lowering the price can become pretty demoralizing. After all, what happens when you lower the price and nothing happens? That can't be too uplifting. Well, some would lower the price again. And again. Eventually you would think that *somebody* would buy it.

2: **Increase the value.** If the perception of the product has a low value, lowering the price won't do much good. The perception of the value has to be raised. Oftentimes, that's difficult to do. To get quicker results, it's better to borrow the perceived value of another product and attach it to the original product. We did just that with the picnics for the Hawaii Winter Baseball League. All you can eat and drink for $25, plus you get a free baseball cap *and* a ticket to a game? That's an offer that's difficult to refuse.

When I started to consult with the New Jersey Nets, I found

them to be the most creative team that I had ever seen—creative in discounting the price of the ticket. I had never seen a team come up with more ways of lowering the price of the ticket.

Every game had been discounted in some way. In fact, one month they featured discounts on milk cartons. "Milk the Nets for Four Bucks," the headline said on the side of the milk carton. Listed were ten games. Some of them were great games, games that featured Michael Jordan or Magic Johnson or Larry Bird. Because the Nets ticket prices were widely discounted and because they had not established a value for those tickets, the "Milk the Nets for Four Bucks" was terrifically *un*successful. The next month, the milk cartons went back to featuring missing children. It's been said that more missing children were found because of the milk cartons than Nets tickets sold.

Instead of lowering the price, we borrowed value from other products to sell tickets at full price. This worked like magic. If you bought a special five-game plan, you got to see the best games—the same type of quality games that had been featured on the milk carton. However, by buying a five-game package, you received a *free gift* for each game in the package. That's five free gifts for each five-game package ordered. The free gifts were a Nets basketball, a Nets cap, a Nets poster, etc. Additionally, there was a different bonus attraction at each of the five games. The Famous Chicken was booked for one of the games, the Bud Light Daredevils for another. We kept on heaping things into these five-game packages to develop something that the fans couldn't refuse.

While the milk carton failed miserably, we sold over 12,000 of these five-game packages for over $1.5 million in new sales. Halfway through this sales effort, one of the seven owners said, "Isn't this *too good* of a deal for the fans?" It wasn't a better financial deal for fans than the "Milk the Nets" deal. That was a fabulous deal—80 percent off the price of the ticket! In the case of the five-game packages, we just took some of the money that would have been deducted by lowering the price and spent it to raise the perceived value of attending a Nets game. Instead of discounting the tickets by 80 percent, we spent about 5 percent of the price of the ticket to add value. And we sold thousands.

You'll see fast-food hamburger chains increase the value of their burgers by tying in with a popular movie like *Batman*. They are borrowing the value of *Batman* to help sell burgers and fries at the regular price. In terms of dollars and cents, a deep discount would be a better deal for the customer. But borrowing the value of *Batman* is a far better deal for the hamburger chain.

It's a better deal for three reasons:

It costs less. A free *Batman* gift is far less costly than a dollar or more discount. The free gift might cost twenty cents. In some cases, the consumer will pay more for the burger, fries, and the "free" gift, thus covering the cost of the gift. The dollar discount always costs a dollar.

You draw more customers away from your competition. Getting a dollar off a burger may not inspire a consumer to switch brands for a day. The dollar discount may go directly to your customers. However, the free gift that is available exclusively at the burger franchise may be a more powerful incentive to draw customers from the competition.

You maintain price integrity. People are still paying the same price for the burger and fries. Sure, they're getting a free gift, but they are conditioning themselves to believe the meal they purchased is a fair deal. They aren't conditioning themselves to only spend 99¢ for a big burger.

3: Lower the price and increase the value. This might seem like a move of desperation. That's okay if it is. Be desperate. But come up with *something* that is too good for the buyer to refuse. We did this once at the New Jersey Nets with huge results.

While we became much better at marketing the better attractions, we still had games that nobody wanted to go to. How exciting was it for our fans when the Los Angeles Clippers came to town to play? The wives and girlfriends of our players didn't even go to this game. It seemed like a flu epidemic had struck only the nieces of Nets players' wives or girlfriends, causing them to miss the Clippers/Nets game. If people who could go to the game for free didn't want to go, how could we get somebody to pay to go?

We took drastic and desperate steps. We lowered the price *and* increased the value. We came up with the White Castle Family Night.

White Castle is a hamburger chain on the East Coast and in the Midwest. The White Castle Family Night was part of their radio sponsorship. There was one White Castle Family Night per month. With this promotion, the consumer would receive:

- Four $16 tickets to a designated Nets game.

- Four meals at White Castle. Since the burgers at White Castle aren't very big, the four meals consisted of twelve hamburgers, four fries, and four Cokes.

- One Nets basketball.

- One Nets cap.

You'd receive all of this for only $39.95 plus postage. Now where else on the East Coast could a family go to a major league sporting event, feed themselves, and get a couple of free gifts for only $39.95? This was over $100 in value for only $39.95.

From the $39.95, we paid White Castle about $10 for each food coupon that was redeemed. We also spent about $2 for a basketball and $1 for a cap. (We were able to get the caps a lot cheaper than at the Hawaii Winter Baseball League, because we ordered 100,000 of them from Taiwan.) Our out-of-pocket expenses were about $13. We kept about $27 per order.

We sold thousands upon thousands of these White Castle Family Nights. In fact, we would usually sell out every game.

For a Nets/Clippers game, we wouldn't have been able to give away tickets. In fact, do you want a pair of tickets? Free. Oh, I'm sorry to hear that your niece is ill. See what I mean? However, when we lowered the price *and* increased the value, we sold out the arena. Our gate receipts for these games were about 100 percent higher than what we would normally have expected.

Using any one of these three tools will cut into your profits. But which is better? Having a great profit margin on a product that no one wants and no one buys or making a real take-it-to-the-bank profit on a product that is selling like crazy?

"THAT'S NOT MARKETING"

"There is another of the ticket packages that I don't like," the director of operations of the Hawaii Winter Baseball League said.

I knew which plan he was referring to. If he thought that our picnic package was "too good" (the one where it was all you could eat and drink for $25 plus a *free* baseball cap and a ticket to the game), then I was sure he wouldn't like the package we designed for the average fan.

"It's too good of a deal for the fan?" I asked.

"Exactly. This is *way* too good of a deal. Outrageous," he said. Then he paused, thinking. "That's not marketing. That's just giving the fan an offer that's too good to refuse."

Exactly! He was finally understanding what jump-start marketing is all about. The product that Hawaiians didn't want was full-season tickets to the Hawaii Winter Baseball League. For a business, the games weren't prestigious enough to woo clients to the ballpark. And why in the world would the average fan want to go to nine home games in nine days during a long home stand?

What they did want was to have a picnic at the ballpark.

What they did want was a ticket package where they didn't have to go to every game and where the offer was too good to refuse. With the second ticket product for Hawaii Winter Baseball, we created a "five-game season ticket." They had tried a similar thing—a six-game package—the year before and it had failed miserably. There was a dollar-a-game discount to buy this package, so six games cost you $30. They sold about 60. Add that to their 100 season tickets, and there were 160 presold tickets to some of the games. Their stadium could hold 4,300 people.

Here's how we repositioned, reshaped, and reconfigured the ticket package:

- You didn't get a dollar-a-game discount. The $6 ticket price wasn't a problem. The price was low enough to where even the homeless could afford it. We felt that a dollar-a-game discount wasn't a motivation to buy. We'd rather spend that dollar to substantially increase the *value* of the ticket package.

- You got only weekend games. Families like to do things on the weekend. Our five-game package featured only weekend games. It worked out to one game every two weeks.

- You got a free Little League baseball bat. If you go to a sporting goods store and buy one, it would cost you about $15. Our cost was $3.50. If you've got a family, which would you prefer: $1 off the ticket or a free $15 Little League bat? For the people who didn't have kids, they probably knew some kids who would love to have a Little League baseball bat.

- You got an official Hawaii Winter Baseball League baseball. In a store, the ball would cost about $7. The league's cost was about $2.

For $30, you would receive tickets to five weekend games plus $22 worth of baseball equipment. This is the type of offer that a fan couldn't refuse. To make this offer cost the Hawaii Winter Baseball league a few cents more than the dollar-a-game discount.

CREATING AN OFFER THAT THEY WILL REFUSE

After I had returned to the mainland, the director of operations convinced the owner of the league that our ticket packages were "too good." He wanted to eliminate the free Little League bat. In other words, he wanted to take a product that nobody wanted and make them an offer that they would refuse. He also got a refusal from me. I, of course, refused to try to market an offer that the consumer would refuse. Heck, anybody can do that.

People don't buy certain products for a reason. It doesn't happen by accident. Jump-start marketing isn't taking a product that nobody wants and cramming it down their throats. It's taking a product that nobody wants and repositioning, reshaping, or reconfiguring it to make it something that a buyer can't refuse.

A Simple Test You Can Take

(Fill in the blanks.) **What are the three tools you have to take a product that nobody wants and turn it into something that a buyer can't refuse?**

A. _____

B. _____

C. _____

(Fill in the blanks.) **Take one of your products that nobody wants to buy and reposition, reshape, or reconfigure it into a product that a buyer can't refuse.**

_____

_____

_____

_____

_____

(Fill in the blanks.) **Now that you've taken a product that nobody wants and turned it into a product they can't refuse, make that product even better. Make it outrageous.**

Answers

1. A. *Lower the price.*

   B. *Increase the value.* You usually do this by borrowing the value of an established product. I prefer this method, because it usually costs less to add value than it does to lower the price. Additionally, when there is added value, the buyer feels like they got a better deal.

   C. *Lower the price and increase the value.* This, of course, is a more desperate measure. You only do this when you're faced with a product like a Nets/Clippers game.

2. Have you really taken a product that nobody wants and turned it into something that they can't refuse?

3. Now you're getting somewhere. This is outrageous! I don't even know what the product is, but I want to buy it.

16. 1,000 WIDOW LADIES

Ground rule #16: Feel free to butt in to other departments.

After each season, pro sports teams send out their season ticket renewal letters. If you had just experienced an awful season, you would sometimes wait until there was some positive news to report, like a trade or the player draft. After an awful season, fans need a "mourning period," then some good news. The great thing about sports is that fans can recover, they have resiliency, and they are eternal optimists.

With the New Jersey Nets, the mourning period became an annual part of the season. We would wait through the mourning period, and then after the player draft, we would send out our season ticket renewal letters.

Before I got to the Nets, about 20 percent of the season ticket holders didn't recover from the previous season, meaning they didn't renew their season tickets. About 60 percent of the season ticket holders, however, were showing life and would send in their deposit before the thirty-day deadline. The remaining 20 percent were tough holdouts.

Because the Nets were always last in the NBA in season tickets, the staff was reluctant to cut off these holdouts. Many of these holdouts would eventually wait to pay until just a week or so before the season started. Some would pay a week or so after the season started. They knew that the Nets would not cancel them.

This was detrimental to the people who had renewed their season tickets earlier. It was detrimental because many of the holdouts had terrific seat locations. If a holdout canceled their season tickets, we gave the option to move into the better seat location to the renewed season ticket holder. However, if the cancellation took place just before the season started, that type of move would be logistically difficult. A *brand-new* season ticket holder would then be assigned to those great seat locations. This, of course, wasn't fair.

I knew we had to change this. I knew we had to somehow find out in a more timely fashion if a holdout season ticket holder was indeed going to pay or was eventually going to cancel. This was not going to be easy, because some of these holdouts had been doing this for years. These people were used to phone calls, which they didn't return. They were used to letters, which they didn't respond to.

Somehow, we had to catch these people's attention without offending them. That's when we went to the rubber chicken.

We purchased a three-foot-long rubber chicken for each of the holdouts. The rubber chicken was placed in a narrow four-foot-long FedEx box. Tell me which holdout season ticket holder wouldn't be curious enough to open that FedEx box.

Now tell me which holdout season ticket holder wouldn't be curious enough to pull that rubber chicken out of the box. When the holdout did that, he would be able to read the little paper basketball tank top that we had put on the chicken's little torso. On the front of the tank top, it said, "Don't fowl out."

On the back of the tank top was this message: "You're about to fowl out! However, you can avoid the bench and keep on playing. Just read the attached."

Attached to the rubber chicken was a letter from me.

Dear Joe:

We have a real problem and we need your help.

We've sent you two renewal notices for your season tickets, and we haven't heard from you. In the past, this situation wasn't really a problem. We would just pester you until the season started. Many times, the season ticket holder would eventually renew; sometimes not.

The "sometimes not" caused the real problem. When a ticket holder told us in September or October that they weren't going to renew, choice seat locations usually opened. These seat locations opened after we had done our upgrading for seat locations for renewed season ticket holders. Thus, brand-new ticket buyers sometimes got terrific seat locations. The result was that people who had been buying from us for years—and who wanted to improve their seat locations—were not served as well as new buyers. Clearly that was unfair.

To change that, we had to determine at an earlier date which season ticket holders were going to renew and which were not. When we knew which seat locations were not renewed, our long-time buyers would then have the option to move to those seats.

Final, Final, Last Gasp Deadline Is July 18

After two renewal mailings, we have sent you our "Don't Fowl Out" mailing. This mailing has our final, final, last gasp deadline of July 18.

To serve our season ticket holders that have renewed, we have set a final, final, last gasp deadline of July 18 for your renewal. Unless you have renewed by that date, we will start moving current season ticket holders into your seats.

We want you to renew your tickets. We think you can have more fun watching us this year than ever before, but we also want to serve those that have renewed. Those that have renewed are our bedrock, and our whole vision has to focus on how to serve them better.

The final, final, last gasp deadline is Monday, July 18. Give us a phone call today.

Best regards,
Jon Spoelstra
President
JS:ls

P.S. If season tickets aren't right for you this year, we've got some other terrific plans that could work for you. To find what is right for you, just call your Nets contact on the enclosed invoice.

The rubber chicken got a marvelous reaction from our holdout season ticket holders! Our renewal rate was the best in New Jersey Nets history—93 percent of our season ticket holders renewed. I can't really attribute this to the rubber chicken, but I do know that it caught the attention of our holdout season ticket holders better than anything we could have done.

Some called up laughing, saying that their check was on its way. Others called and asked if they could have another chicken to show their friends. I even got calls from paid-up season ticket holders who felt cheated because they didn't receive a rubber chicken. (I sent them one.)

Only one caller was a little perturbed. I got a call from a holdout season ticket holder who was a doctor originally from India. His English was certainly passable, but I think he missed some of the American nuances of my rubber chicken mailing.

He said, "I opened your box in front of a bunch of nurses. I thought it might have been a souvenir. Why did you send me a dead duck?"

■

If you were stretched out on a couch, you could get a shrink to put down his pencil and paper and really listen if you told him this, "I walked into a nightmare, used jump-start marketing, and was catapulted into another entirely different nightmare."

"Hmm. . . . Tell me about it," the shrink might say.

The "nightmare-into-nightmare" happened to me at the New Jersey Nets. In my first year as a consultant with the Nets, we sold ticket packages in such quantities that we didn't have the ability to process them in a timely manner. In other words, we outsold our ability to produce.

Many companies *think* they would like to have that problem. But once you're in the midst of this type of nightmare, you meet up with another type of frustration. Worst of all, for each one of these new sales that you have created, the "back room" has created a dissatisfied customer.

WHY IT WILL HAPPEN, AUTOMATICALLY, EVERY TIME

Who are these bad guys in the back room, anyway? Why are they wrecking your sales?

Depending on the type of company, the back room could be manufacturing, assembling, or, as in the case of the Nets, fulfilling the order with already printed tickets. The back room could also include parts of the financial wing, particularly billing and collecting.

Once the jump-start sales start coming through, you can be guaranteed that a Chinese fire drill will occur in the back room. I'm not really sure that you can avoid it. Let's take a look at why the back room will be slow to adapt to jump-start marketing:

1: The back room has adjusted itself to pre-jump-start marketing. Whatever your pace of sales has been, the back room has adjusted to it to make sure they don't finish processing orders too quickly. If you process orders too quickly, the back room is ripe for layoffs. After all, what manager is going to sit by and watch the back room play cards or otherwise whittle away the day because the back room processed the orders too quickly? The only insurance that the back room has is to process the orders at a slower pace and look busy while doing it. That's the "law of the back room."

2: Inefficient back room systems. It would be suicide for the back room to initiate, on its own, more efficient systems in processing orders. More efficient systems violate the law of the back room, which would lead to layoffs.

The back room can adjust to a spurt in sales. There's enough elasticity built in so that the workers can speed up the processing a bit without causing a Chinese fire drill. However, when there is an avalanche of new orders, the whole inefficient system freezes.

Before we started jump-start marketing with the Nets, I surveyed the Nets box office, the place where they would process tickets. The box office was highly inefficient, of course. That wasn't unusual—this is standard for pro sports teams. After talking with the people in the box office, I felt that they had a good work ethic and that they would be up to the challenge. But was I wrong!

As the blizzard of orders came in, they were stacked on the floor. The stack reached about six feet in height, then they started another stack. The box office worked long hours to get through those stacks, but the next day more orders were placed on top of the slowly shrinking stacks. Thus, the first order that came in was at the bottom of the stack. At the bottom of the stack, that first order would be the last one to be processed. First in, last out. In other words, the customer who ordered first would get the worst seat location.

That process was changed a bit, by accident. Somebody bumped into the stacks, and the stacks came tumbling down, scattering all over. The stacks were immediately rebuilt to resemble the original stacks in height. About the only order that stayed constant was the first one, the one at the bottom of the stack.

When the ticket orders weren't processed in an orderly fashion, either the salesperson or the customer called the box office in search of the tickets. With stacks and stacks of orders to process, the box office people weren't in the best mood to search through the stacks, thus they often took out their frustration either on the people who sold the orders or the people who had bought the tickets—and sometimes on both.

RESENTING JUMP-START MARKETING

The more orders, the more the back room is going to resent jump-start marketing. The increase in orders is good for the company, but the back room doesn't see it as good for them. After all, they have to process more orders for the same pay. They yearn for the good old days before jump-start marketing. With the increase in customer dissatisfaction, their yearnings might come to reality.

The boss of the back room will, of course, request more people to handle the orders. That's law number two of the back room: request more full-time employees. Nothing is said about making it a more efficient place. That is not part of the thought process when orders are piling up like snowflakes in a blizzard.

Jump-start marketing won't end with the initial rush of orders. The more the principles of jump-start marketing are used, the more sophisticated the employees become in jump-start marketing. In other words, the problems in the back room will not go away. Knowing that the problems won't go away, there is a two-step process to make the back room a marketing tool instead of a source of customer dissatisfaction. It starts with 1,000 widow ladies.

1,000 WIDOW LADIES

These two steps have to be done simultaneously:

1: **Hire 1,000 widow ladies part-time today.** Seeing the mess in the Nets box office, I vowed that we would hire 1,000 widow ladies if we had to get out from under all those ticket orders. I used that phrase more as a colorful way of saying that we had to do whatever was necessary to attack those piles of orders. What we couldn't do was increase the burden on those people in the box office. Right away, we needed to add temporary workers, whether they be widow ladies or not.

Every day that we waited, there would be hundreds of fans getting angrier and angrier. They could easily become a terrorist group. Sales are much too difficult to achieve to see the benefits of those sales flushed away by an inefficient back room.

2: Start today on creating a more efficient system. Unfortunately, a lasting, more efficient system can't be created and installed in one day. The back room had been working for years in making the system inefficient, and now they were being asked to make it a slick, well-oiled system? No way. Any changes or tinkering with the system will take a hammer-and-tong battle. To handle the increase in sales from jump-start marketing, there will have to be new systems in the back room.

The hiring of the 1,000 widow ladies should take care of the short-term problems of the back room. However, the 1,000 widow ladies should be considered a Band-Aid, a temporary solution. The real solution is to change the system in the back room, and that will take time.

With the Nets, we quickly realized that the computer ticketing system that we were using was totally inadequate to handle the higher volume of orders. Changing to a different computer program—and hardware—is not an overnight job. When we looked at the six different vendors that provided computer ticketing software, we found severe deficiencies in each. It seems that the software was written by people in the back room. The software made their jobs a little more convenient, but none of the programs helped in the marketing process.

At one meeting discussing our options, I said, "Aw, the heck with it. Let's write our own." This is where you can find the back room striking back.

One of the back roomers said, "It's impossible to write a

computer program from scratch." Interesting. I'm glad that our back roomer never had a conversation with Bill Gates and Paul Allen when they were first fiddling around with writing software code.

We wanted our ticketing software to be "president-proof"— you know, like in idiot-proof. It took us a few months to find the right software-writing company. When we did, we were off to the races in creating back-room software that actually enhanced the marketing process.

IF YOU FEEL YOU BELONG, BUTT IN

There used to be a quaint Irish bar in Chicago named Hobson's Oyster Bar. Hobson's served the best crab gumbo in the history of the world. Inside, there was a long bar and only three booths. Above the booths was a sign: THE FOOD IS HERE FOR THE CONVENIENCE OF THE DRINKERS. Jim Dowling, the owner, had figured out which customers contributed the most to the profit. He didn't want his booths and bar stools filled with light drinkers enjoying that terrific crab gumbo. He wanted those high-profit drinkers two deep at the bar waiting for one of the booths to open up.

In remembrance of Hobson's, I draw a parallel to the back room. The back room is there for the convenience of the jump-start marketers and their customers. How does the back room become a convenience of the customers?

Before we overloaded the Nets box office with orders, we had initiated a new policy: All ticket orders would be processed within eight hours. With prompt processing, the customer would get their tickets two or three days after the order was placed. That's very unusual for teams. It's a benefit, of course, to the customer.

However, it seems that a lot of times the back room thinks that they are there for the convenience of themselves. In these back rooms, the work is done, but at a pace and methodology that is friendly only to those in the back room. Jump-start marketing naturally extends to the back room. If the "front room" doesn't recognize this, then each of the jump-start marketing principles will become a little less effective. If the back room isn't friendly, efficient, and customer-oriented, the jump-start executive needs to butt in. Neither the jump-start marketer nor the company can afford for the executive *not* to butt in.

A Simple Test You Can Take

(True or False.) **The back room is essential to jump-start marketing.**

True　　False

(True or False.) **Hiring 1,000 widow ladies is a long-term solution.**

True　　False

(True or False.) **It would be a popular move for the jump-start executive to butt in to the running of the back room.**

True　　False

Answers

1: *True.* In the short-term, a jump-start marketing company can get by with a back room that is . . . well . . . backward. But it's silly to think that the jump-start techniques will continue to flourish if the back room doesn't respond.

2: *False.* Hiring 1,000 widow ladies is inefficient and cumbersome. In the short-term, it is a better alternative than getting the orders out late. It provides a cushion while remaking the back room into a friendly, efficient department.

3: *False.* Departments are naturally protective. The back room isn't going to hold an Easter parade for the jump-start marketer who butts in. Sure, there will be resentment. But it is absolutely, positively necessary that the back room help jump-start marketing, not impede it.

17. CHOOSE WHICH CUSTOMER TO DUMP

Ground rule #17: Differentiate between big and little customers.

NATURE'S LAW #1: IF YOU WIN, FANS WILL COME

This law sounds logical, but it is wrong.

Sure, it's far better for a pro sports team to win games, but if you do win, it doesn't automatically mean that fans will come. I gave examples of this in chapter 2. An example that strikes closer to home for me is the 1994–95 season in northern New Jersey.

During that season, the New Jersey Devils in the NHL were terrific all season long, and they handily won the Stanley Cup. The Nets were awful, struggling to win just thirty of eighty-two games. Yet the Nets had a higher attendance during that season than the world champion New Jersey Devils.

Well, how about the next season? Winning the Stanley Cup should have brought a deluge of new-ticket business for the Devils. It did. It brought about $3 million in new ticket business. The poor Nets? During that same summer, the Nets faced the summer of the lock-out. The NBA was negotiating with the players' association for a new agreement. During the negotiations, teams were not allowed to use player names or pictures of players. After winning only thirty games, you might think that was a marketing advantage to us. But since we couldn't promote Michael Jordan or The Shaq, it was a terrible handicap. We did only $4 million in new ticket business. That was $1 million more in new ticket business than the Stanley Cup champions.

So scratch Nature's Law #1.

NATURE'S LAW #2: IF YOU LOSE, ALL THE CUSTOMER SERVICE IN THE WORLD WON'T KEEP THE FANS COMING TO THE GAMES

Again, winning is better. The best marketing is to win five championships in a span of seven years, like the Edmonton Oilers did in the NHL.

But this law is wrong, too.

The Edmonton Oilers felt that winning was everything, that winning was the best way to market, that all the customer service in the world won't keep fans coming to the games if you're no longer winning. They proved themselves right. Except that they were wrong.

Each year that they won a Stanley Cup, they would see their season ticket numbers *decrease.* Alarm bells should have rung. Warning flags should have popped up. However, they thought that winning would solve those problems. The slide continued. Just a few years after their last championship, they were in deep financial trouble.

During my eleven years at the Portland Trail Blazers, I didn't want that to happen to us. During my tenure, unlike the Edmonton Oilers, we didn't win championships. In fact, we were just an average team. We'd win only a few more games than we would lose.

However, we sold out every home game during my eleven years there. Part of that I attribute to customer service.

Customer service is not something you expect in dealing with a sports team. If you've ever bought tickets at an arena's box office, you know that ticket sellers are famous for being rude to fans. In Portland, we went the opposite direction. I'll give you an example:

One of our season ticket holders called up our customer service department. He said, "My tickets are locked in my desk, I'm out of town, and I've promised them to a key client coming in from out of town."

This type of call usually happened about an hour before the game. We keyed the customer's name into the computer. Let's say it was Mr. Jones. We also got the seat location.

"Where was your client going to pick up your tickets, Mr. Jones?" our fan satisfaction CEO would ask. (We had renamed our customer service department the fan satisfaction department. Each person had the title of CEO, because they had the power and the glory to solve any problem.)

"He wasn't," Mr. Jones replied, "I was going to have them delivered to his hotel."

"No problem. I can call over there and have him paged. I'll let him know that duplicate tickets will be left for him at the VIP will-call window. Or, if you prefer, I'll call your client and have the tickets cabbed over to him."

"The cab sounds like a good idea. Can you bill me for that?"

"Of course not, Mr. Jones. We're glad we could help you out."

We would write out a ticket voucher for replacement tickets for that one game. If it cost us $10 to cab the tickets over to the client, that was fine with us. After all, this didn't happen to every season ticket holder for every game. This added up to about $20 worth every season. By spending $20, we practically insured season ticket renewals worth $20,000.

If we would have spent $10 on every account—like buying a Portland Trail Blazer baseball cap and giving it to each account—the results wouldn't have nearly as much impact. We weren't just spending $10 on Mr. Jones, we were solving a problem that he felt was important.

We went on being mediocre as a team. For the fun of it, I tracked Mr. Jones's account each year. In five years, he had spent over $60,000 with us. Who knows, he might have continued renewing his season tickets, anyway. But each year when it came down to renewing his season tickets, you can bet that we had something going for us on our side besides a mediocre team. We had a good memory sitting on Mr. Jones's shoulder like a guardian angel.

■

To illustrate a point in this chapter, I was thinking of different things that are *easy* to do in business. For instance, it's really pretty easy *not* to speak up during a meeting with more than ten people in the room. It's also pretty easy to at least think about *not* taking your vacation as your getaway day comes closer and closer. Why do crises always seem to pop up just a day or so before you're going to leave? Although it doesn't happen often, it's easy to spill a cup of coffee on an airplane en route to an important meeting.

The easiest thing in business, however, is losing regular customers. This can be done without even thinking. It can be done without even a modicum of effort. You can just sit there and do it.

As we know, getting a new customer takes a lot of work. While jump-start marketing makes it a little easier, getting new customers still takes thinking. It takes effort.

From personal experience at the New Jersey Nets, I know how difficult it is to get customers. On a scale of one-to-ten—

with one being the easiest and ten being the toughest—getting customers for the New Jersey Nets ranks as a twelve. Perhaps as high as a fifteen.

As a consultant, I worked with companies that had difficulty in getting new customers. The degree of difficulty in getting new customers with some of these companies would grade as a nine. Compared to the Nets, that may seem easy, but getting customers is never easy. I have never once said that it was easy, even to myself.

Knowing how difficult it is to get customers, I'm always amazed at how easy companies make it to get rid of them. I'm not talking about getting rid of them *on purpose*. I'm referring to letting good customers get stolen by the competition or just plain slip away.

MINDLESS DUMPING OF CUSTOMERS

I've come to the conclusion that companies inadvertently choose which customers to let go. Unfortunately, the customers that these companies choose are rarely the small customers. It's usually the bigger customers. It's not that these companies search out their bigger customers and dump them. It's just that these companies haven't developed a system of which customers to dump.

Using the principles of jump-start marketing will get new business. To feel the full effects of jump-start marketing, we don't want that new business to replace the business that is lost. We want to be able to *add* that new business on top of what we have. To do that, we have to have a system of which business to dump. This system doesn't allow the customer to choose to dump us or not. *We* choose which customers to dump.

YOUR CHOICE

Companies choose the wrong customers to let go because of two reasons. If you're a mid-level or upper level executive, you'll probably feel that these two reasons don't apply to you. Don't try to suppress those feelings. Just think as you read, How stupid some of these poor companies are. After reading this chapter, I'd recommend that you reread chapter 10. Experiment with some of the principles in that chapter. When you experiment with those principles, you'll find that you are closer to your customers and, unfortunately, the two reasons in this chapter hit a little closer to home. You'll find that your company is a little bit stupid. You'll find that your company chose to let customers go without even thinking about it.

Here are the two reasons:

- **Not differentiating between big and little customers.** The airlines have figured this out the best with their frequent-flyer programs. Since I fly over 100,000 miles a year on United Airlines, I get beyond-the-call-of-duty service. It extends to almost the extreme. For instance, on long flights the flight attendant will deliver to me the business card of the captain of the plane. On the back, he will have written and signed a short thank-you note for choosing their airline.

  With the personal attention, the free trips, and the free upgrades, I feel I have a vested interest in flying United. It would be difficult for me to change to another airline. That doesn't apply to the credit card company that I use to pay for all those trips.

  With all that traveling, it is a chore to keep track of my expenses. To make it a little easier, I came up with a system. It's not very complicated—I dedicated one Visa charge card for business expenses. Last year, I charged over $50,000 on that Visa card.

You would think that the bank that issued the Visa card could differentiate me as a good customer. Heck, a lot of other banks seem to. It seems that every day I receive a new mailing from a bank about how terrific their Visa card is. I hope these banks don't put a $100 bill in their mailing. I throw away each one unopened. Lately, however, I've been opening them and actually reading the copy. I'm going to switch. Why? My "Big Bank" Visa card company doesn't differentiate between its customers.

Here's how they failed to differentiate.

On a rare night at home, I received a phone call from a woman at "Big Bank." She said that they hadn't received last month's payment. I knew, of course, that I had paid it. I always pay the full amount when I get the bill. However, I dutifully looked into my checkbook. Sure enough, I had paid it. But they hadn't received it. As I talked, I found myself thinking, This sure sounds like I'm using the old "in-the-mail" trick.

The "Big-Bank" woman said they were suspending my charge privileges until they got at least the minimum amount, which was $70. This got me thinking.

Trying to sound like a friendly professor and not like a deadbeat, I asked, "Do you have my account information in front of you on the computer?"

"Yes," she replied.

"Am I one of your better customers?"

"I can't answer that," she replied.

"Well, let's assume for the moment that I am. Let's assume that not everybody charges $50,000 a year."

Silence.

"You're going to cut me off because of $70?"

"Yes."

"Even though I'm one of your better customers?"

"We don't give one customer better treatment than the others," she said. "We treat everyone the same."

I thought about that. The bank's marketing department in charge of getting new customers certainly doesn't treat everybody the same. When they buy a mailing list, they set certain parameters for those names like income, age, etc. Wouldn't they do the same for existing customers? When an account is delinquent, wouldn't the computer flag the bigger accounts for special treatment? I tried to find out.

I wrote the president of the bank a letter. Two weeks later I received a reply from the assistant to the assistant. Was there an ivory tower complex here? The assistant to the assistant wrote that my letter was being forwarded to customer service. The VP-customer service wrote a letter that basically said they had rules to follow. In other words, if you don't pay $70, see ya.

Rules? Do rules really apply to bigger customers? Of course not. Bigger customers are too hard to get. The only rule that should apply to bigger customers is:

Find out what the problem is and help fix it.

In my case, "Big Bank" wasn't interested in the problem. They were interested in the $70. The cost of that interest was $50,000. If "Big Bank" would have used my one rule, the conversation would have gone like this:

"I mailed the payment on December 7," I would say.
"At this time, Mr. Spoelstra, we haven't received it," the "Big Bank" customer service person would say.
"But the Christmas mails can sometimes slow things

down. We'll wait for the mails. Another week should do it. In the meantime, your new bill is about to arrive. When it does, please pay it as you usually do. It probably won't reflect your payment of December 7, so just pay the current amount minus the check you wrote on December 7. If your check doesn't come, I'll call you back and recommend that you cancel the first check and just write a new one."

Why give that type of service? Doesn't it cost money in manpower and phone lines to provide that type of service? Sure it does. But what type of manpower and money does it cost to get a new $50,000 account? It costs far more to get the new big customer than it does to find out what a current customer's problem is and *help* fix it.

In the case of "Big Bank," they didn't differentiate between big and little customers. I'm not saying that the smaller customers should be treated like dirt. Each customer should be treated superbly. However, bigger customers should be treated *more superbly.* If you've got hundreds or thousands or tens of thousands of customers, how do you differentiate the bigger customers? With "Big Bank," it would be pretty easy. All they would have to do is have a warning flag pop up on their computers whenever communication was necessary to the bigger customers. When this flag popped up, it would be time to use the "more superb" service.

- **Treating everybody as if they are a scam artist.** You may think that this point is very similar to the first point. I admit, it's a bit related.

  Even though there have been hundreds of books written about customer service, I find more and more companies dealing with customers as if they were scam artists. This happened when I first arrived as a consultant to the New Jersey Nets.

I wandered into the Nets box office one day. Besides filling ticket orders, these people were the customer service department. On this day, a woman from that department was in a heavy debate on the phone. I stood there and listened. Finally, she said to the customer, "Can I put you on hold for a minute?"

She looked at me. "What would you do?" she asked. "This guy is trying to rip us off." I was surprised that she was so negatively passionate about this. She was a delightful person with a charming personality. Except on this phone call.

She quickly told me the problem. This fan had purchased eight tickets to one game. For whatever reason, he couldn't go. To make things worse, he had lost the tickets. He wanted to trade these lost tickets in for eight tickets to another game. His request sure took guts! Anybody in the ticket business knows that if you don't use your tickets for an event, you lose them. And if you lose your tickets, you've *really* lost them.

"Give him eight tickets to another game," I said.

"What! He's trying to rip us off!" she protested.

"Let him," I said. "Let him rip us off."

This woman allowed us to get ripped off and offered the fan eight tickets to one game. Afterward, we talked.

"How do you know this guy was trying to rip us off? Do you know him?" I asked.

"I could just tell," she said.

"What if he was a legit customer? It's almost impossible to tell over the phone who is a scam artist and who is a legit customer. Why be the judge?"

I asked her how many incidents she got in a season that she would judge as "scams."

She thought and said, "About twenty."

"Let them scam us," I said. "We've got 250,000 tickets that we *didn't* sell last season, so if you gave 10 to each *scam* artist, we'd still have 249,800 tickets to sell."

Instead of the box-office people acting as judge and jury, we wanted them to act as marks. You know, marks are the victims that scam artists cheat.

"If the same name pops up, let me know. Or, if these scam artists put out instructions on the Internet about how to get tickets from the Nets, we'll find out. In the meantime, let's get ripped off."

When the Nets box-office people started to act as naive marks, their customer service quotient exploded to the top of the graph. They were giving away tickets to *every* problem. They were becoming heroes. We kept track of how many tickets we gave away. It was less than 2,000 for the season. We still had 248,000 tickets to sell.

I tracked that fan that "scammed" us out of eight tickets. In fact, over the years, I got to know him a bit. Before he bought season tickets from me for about $8,000, he had purchased over $10,000 in tickets during a three-season time frame.

Did he actually scam us out of eight tickets? Who cares! Over the next four seasons, he had purchased $18,000 worth of tickets from the Nets. The way our team had been playing, you might ask the question, "Who scammed who?"

BUILDING A POLICY MANUAL IN TEN SECONDS

The woman in the box office told me, "Even though it bothers me to give away tickets to scam artists, I will do it. But we need a policy manual for these occasions."

I agreed. I borrowed her pen and a piece of paper and began to write.

When I was finished writing, I pulled off a piece of tape from her tape dispenser and taped the page up on the wall.

The page said:

Find out what the problem is and *help* fix it.

"That's it?" she asked. "That's our policy manual?"

"That's it," I said.

So now you can see how the two points are related. I don't like to lose *any* customer. However, losing customers does happen. Customers can move away. Customers can lose their jobs because of downsizing. And, unfortunately, customers can die. When a Portland Trail Blazer season ticket holder died and we found out about it in a timely fashion, we usually sent flowers. This wasn't for marketing purposes, it was being a caring company.

Companies can't stop losing customers, but they can stop losing big customers if they differentiate them from little customers. Losing big customers really hurts. It hurts the bottom line immediately, and it diminishes the true results that you can get from jump-start marketing. What hurts the worst is losing a big customer without really knowing why.

A Simple Test You Can Take

(Fill in the blanks.) **List the two reasons companies choose to dump the wrong customer.**

A. _____

B. _____

(Fill in the blank.) **What is the one rule for dealing with big customers?**

_____

Answers

1. The two reasons that companies choose to dump the wrong customer are:

   A. *That companies fail to differentiate between big and little customers.* It's stupid to think that all customers are equal, just as it's stupid to think that all employees are equal. We're not talking about human rights here. We're talking about importance to the business. For instance, suppose one sales employee is a superstar, but is habitually late to meetings. That superstar isn't fired for being late. Another employee might be. There is more slack cut for the bigger producers of a company, whether it be a customer or an employee. Not seeing that, not differentiating the big customer from the little customer or the sales superstar from the slug might seem fair and equitable, but it is bad business.

   B. *Treating every customer as if they were a scam artist.* I like my cure for this. Be a naive mark. Let the customer win. After doing this for awhile, companies will find that they enjoy being a naive mark and that fewer and fewer customers seem as if they are scam artists.

2. Find out what the problem is and help fix it. This, of course, works for all customers. With big customers, you have to add a little flair to the problem solving. For example, let's take my example of "Big Bank." Instead of getting a letter back from the

assistant to the assistant, what if I would have received a letter from the person that I wrote to, the bank president. Since I had taken the time to write to the president, it seems appropriate that he answer me. Sure, I know he's busy. But so am I, and I took the time. Easily, an assistant could have written the letter, had the president sign it, and say that it was being handed over to the VP-customer service. The only thing different from the assistant to the assistant's letter and a president's letter would be the signature. And a P.S. The president's letter could have said that if there were any future problems, be sure to communicate with him.

I might have *thought* that the president hadn't even seen my letter and that an assistant answered it for him, but I wouldn't have *known*. After awhile, I probably would have convinced myself that the president personally wrote the letter. Would I have dumped "Big Bank"? Of course not. The president and I were good buddies, we were pen pals.

18. WHEN WILL YOU STOP?

Ground rule #18: When the going gets rough, increase expenses that are not fixed, like salespeople.

The Spanish professional basketball league (ACB) asked me if I would give an all-day marketing seminar to the owners of the teams in Barcelona, Spain. I agreed.

To overcome the language differences, the ACB hired the personal interpreter of the president of Spain. He sat in a soundproof room behind me, and each of the owners had an earpiece. As I spoke, the interpreter would translate on the fly. My feeling is that he did a marvelous job.

I base this on humor. If a person can translate humor, then the interpreter can translate anything. I tested the interpreter early. I threw out a couple of one-liners and watched the audience react. If they just sat there, then I could figure that either the one-liners weren't funny or the interpreter fumbled it. The audience laughed, and we were off and running.

Pro sports teams outside the United States basically lack one thing that the American pro teams have: marketing. This is true throughout the world, whether it be Spain, Japan, or Brazil. The

ACB is the second-best run basketball league in the world behind the NBA, but each team needed to beef up its marketing.

To make that point, I tried to encourage each team to hire at least one ticket salesperson. Most foreign teams believe that if the fan wants to come to a game, the fan will come. In today's economics, with player salaries the way they are, that belief no longer work. Teams throughout the world have to be marketed.

To underscore this, I brought out a roll of pesetas. I held out a 100 peseta bill and asked, "Who will give me 10 pesetas for this 100 peseta bill?"

The Spaniards looked at me as if I were crazy. Or maybe the interpreter fumbled it.

I asked again, "Who will give me 10 pesetas for this 100 peseta bill?" I walked around the room waving the bill.

One team owner reached into his pocket and pulled out a 10 peseta coin and held it up. I jumped on it. When the exchange was made, I asked him if he had another 10 peseta coin. If he did, I would give him another 100 peseta bill. I waved it in front of me.

He retrieved another 10 peseta coin and we made the exchange. By the time I pulled out another 100 peseta bill, he had another 10 peseta coin in his hand ready for the exchange. The other owners now had 10 peseta coins in their hands, laughing, wanting to take advantage of this crazy American.

I made the exchange with the same Spaniard three more times. Then I asked, "When will you stop giving me 10 peseta coins for 100 peseta bills?"

I held up the roll of 100 peseta bills.

He said, "I will keep on giving you 10 peseta coins until you don't have 100 peseta bills left."

"Correct," I said. "Right answer!"

"Then why would you not hire a ticket salesperson?" I asked. "That ticket salesperson will give you 100 peseta bills and keep just a 10 peseta coin. That ticket salesperson will keep on giving you 100 peseta bills all year long, and your cost is only one 10 peseta coin for each 100 peseta bill you receive.

"In fact, why would you not hire two ticket salespeople? Now you would have two people giving you 100 peseta bills. Why not three ticket salespeople . . . "

Some of the owners in the room got the message. A year later, the ACB sent me their attendance figures from each team. The teams that had hired ticket salespeople all had huge increases of 50 percent or more. Not one team that didn't hire a ticket salesperson had an increase of over 5 percent.

The owner that got all of my 100 peseta bills hired *three* ticket salespeople. In the year to come, he got more new 100 peseta bills than anyone in the room, and all he gave out for it was 10 peseta coins. At the end of his season, he sent me a fax telling me he had mailed me two packages.

One package arrived on a Friday. Inside was a framed 100 peseta bill. Under the 100 peseta bill was an engraving. It said, "I didn't stop. Thank you."

I felt great about receiving that framed 100 peseta bill. But what in the world could be in the second package? Like an old man waiting for his mail with nothing else to do, I waited.

Finally, Monday came. The other package had another framed 100 peseta bill. This one was engraved, "I applied your strategy to my own business and I didn't stop here, either. Thank you."

■

A minor league hockey team felt that they couldn't afford ticket salespeople. Not even one. Then they decided to play one game in a new and much larger arena in their town. They spent $60,000 advertising that one game, and the fans came. Instead of the normal 5,000 or so in attendance, they had

9,000. At an average price of $8 a ticket, their gate for that one game increased $32,000.

The owner asked my opinion.

I said, "If you would have spent that $60,000 on acquiring salespeople, you probably would have increased your sales by $600,000 for the season."

Which would you prefer: $600,000 or $32,000?

While I've used sports teams as examples here, I find similar thinking in businesses in other industries. Like pro sports teams, other industries have fixed costs. With a pro sports team, the major fixed cost is the product—in this case, the players. The cost of players could reach 70 percent of the total revenue of the team. The fixed cost in other industries is also the product, whatever that product may be.

Somewhere along the line, every company needs to do some financial belt-tightening. Most likely, they've whittled and squeezed costs out of manufacturing their products. These are, of course, their fixed costs, because without a product there is no company.

It's a little bit different with pro sports. There is usually no whittling and squeezing of expenses out of the product. In fact, the professional sports leagues have some sort of team salary cap to keep the product costs down. However, almost every general manager of a team stays up nights trying to figure out ways of circumventing the salary cap so that they can spend *more* on the product. I have never met a general manager who has stayed up even one night to figure out a way of lowering product costs.

With financial belt-tightening, a company or a pro sports team will automatically focus on the nonfixed costs. In many cases, this usually means sales and marketing people.

SPENDING TO OBLIVION; CUTTING SALESPEOPLE

I have consulted with teams that have the "spending to oblivion" mentality. The team will have just spent $1.3 million on a third-string player, but the owner will say that they can't afford $50,000 to bolster their sales staff. If anything, they have to cut a young salesperson, which translates to about $20,000 in costs. This thinking doesn't just border on the ridiculous, it fully falls into the abyss of bona fide big-league stupidity. And pro sports teams aren't the only companies that take that plunge.

"Our sales are down," one company executive told me while we exchanged secrets on a long plane ride.

"What are you doing about it?" I asked.

"We're tightening our belt. For instance, the only way I can fly first-class is that I'm using some of my award checks," the executive said. "And, oh yeah, we're cutting back on our sales staff and our marketing expenses."

I wondered if he worked for a pro sports team.

WHEN THE GOING GETS ROUGH, INCREASE YOUR NONFIXED EXPENSES (SALESPEOPLE)

To make a point, sometimes it takes an absurd example. That's the case here. I'm going to use Major League Baseball to make a point about how when the going gets rough, it's time to increase your nonfixed expenses. That's right: When the going gets rough, *increase* your nonfixed expenses.

My absurdity example started in October of 1994, when there was no World Series. The owners were trying to lower their fixed costs by putting in a salary cap for the players. That part isn't absurd. Major League teams were perfect examples of spending themselves into oblivion. The players, of course, refused to even negotiate that point. Thus, no late season pennant race, no World Series.

The stalemate lasted throughout the winter and into spring. No spring training. The media were predicting that there might not even be a season at all in 1995. What's a team to do, what's a team to do?

Most baseball teams zeroed in on a portion of their nonfixed expenses or nonplayer expenses. These teams didn't target their finance or PR departments, nor did they target the executives. The bull's-eye was the ticket salespeople. In many cases, they laid off the entire sales department. With no baseball, there wasn't a need for a ticket sales staff. When the going gets rough, *decrease* your nonfixed expenses. Logical thinking, right?

Well, a Major League Baseball team does most of its marketing in the off-season. When the baseball season is over, the nuts-and-bolts marketing starts for the *next* season. In fact, in many cases 80 percent of a team's ticket revenue is sold during the solid six months of off-season.

A month or so after the World Series wasn't played, an owner of a Major League Baseball team called me for advice. At the time, I was president of the New Jersey Nets.

"*Increase* your sales staff," I said.

"What?" he said. He probably didn't think he was hearing me right.

"*Increase* your sales staff," I repeated. "Eventually, there will be baseball. If you go through the winter months without selling tickets, you're facing losses in the millions and millions."

"But the way negotiations are going, we might miss a lot of the 1995 season. Who is going to buy tickets knowing that? Who can sell under that handicap?"

Yes, the going was indeed rough. "What your fans need is a guarantee. You have to take the risk off of the fans' backs.

With a guarantee, you would have something to market."

The NBA itself was going through some difficult negotiating with the players' association. If there was going to be a work stoppage of some sort, we at the Nets had already figured out our strategy. We were going to make a guarantee to our fans:

Prime-rate interest for each game that wasn't played. If games were missed because of a work stoppage, we were going to refund the money that our season ticket holders (and other ticket-package buyers) had paid us *plus prime-rate interest.* The interest would be computed from the time that they had paid us in full to the time we cut the check for any unplayed games.

When the work stoppage became a real threat and our guarantee was in place, one season ticket holder called me up and asked me what I thought the chances were that the entire season would be missed.

I asked why.

"Well, prime-rate interest is better than what I can get on my own. If the entire season is going to be missed, I just might want to buy some more season tickets."

I explained to the baseball team owner what we were thinking about. I then did some quick math over the phone. The quick math showed that the guarantee would cost peanuts to a baseball team, because the prime-rate interest per game worked out to only 25¢ per $15 ticket per game. If the baseball work stoppage lasted the entire eighty-one home game season, the season ticket holder would receive $20.25 in interest for each season ticket.

That's really cheap insurance. It's a cheap cost to acquire credibility in a noncredible labor situation.

"With a guarantee, the salespeople would *now* have something to sell. If there is baseball, terrific. The fans have what they want—baseball. If there are games missed, the fans aren't hurt financially. In fact, they *gain*."

There was silence on the end of the phone.

Finally, the owner said, "I'm thinking."

Some more silence.

"We're talking about replacement players," the owner blurted out. "You know, scabs, guys that didn't play professional baseball anyplace last year."

"How about another guarantee?" I said. Now he must have thought I was really crazy. "With this guarantee, the fan would only pay the full price of the ticket if the majority of the major league players were playing. If it's scabs, there would be a dramatic rebate. After all, with scabs, you wouldn't have the multimillion-dollar contracts. Now you're back selling tickets again. However, even with these guarantees, selling will be more difficult because of all the negative media about the negotiations. I think you'll have to increase your sales staff just to stay even with last year. But at least you'll be making sales."

More silence.

"I'd like to think about your suggestions," the owner said. "I'll call you back in a few days with more questions."

The call never came. This owner had done what the other Major League Baseball owners did. He didn't increase his ticket sales staff. He laid them all off.

In April of 1995, a federal court ordered baseball to be played. The teams scrambled to put together an abbreviated and late spring training. This late spring training was after the time frame when thousands of "snow birds" had visited Florida and Arizona in hopes of seeing their favorite team prepare for the regular season. Two weeks after this make-good spring training, the official season started. In that two-week period, teams were scrambling to put together a sales staff. In that two-week period, the quickly assembled sales staff had to produce sales numbers that normally took six months.

When baseball abruptly started, many baseball teams had a decline of season tickets of 40 percent. These teams had laid off the ticket sales staff. Thus, there was no sales staff to work with the season ticket holder who had received his renewal bill. The only things there were the season ticket renewal bill and a ton of negative publicity. There was also no sales staff to sell *new* season tickets to replace those that couldn't be renewed.

The team whose owner called me up usually sold 400,000 group tickets during a season. About 90 percent of those sales are made in the off-season. When the season started, not one group ticket had been sold. They eventually sold about 100,000 group tickets at highly discounted prices. The revenue flowed downward from about $3 million in group ticket sales to less than $600,000.

The media reported that the team lost about $15 million during the 1995 season. The expense of a sales staff for the entire *year* was only about $500,000, including commissions, benefits, everything. Beefing up the sales staff might have cost another $100,000.

It turned out to be a case of pay me now or pay me later. In this case, it was pay about $600,000 for a sales staff or *$15 million* without one.

WHEN THE GOING GETS ROUGH OR THE GOING GETS GREAT

It seems in vogue now that when things get rough, lay people off. That, of course, is the ninety-day-wonder approach that may temporarily appease Wall Street. In some cases, these company CEOs consider that grabbing an ax and whacking employees is the macho thing to do. It's respected by Wall Street. The CEO feels confident that laying people off is the smart and safe thing to do. However, except in the most dire situations, laying people off usually just obscures the problem—*lack of revenue.* This lack of revenue is usually blamed on something other than the CEO. The economy is usually easy to blame, and, after awhile, the CEO and others actually believe that it is the economy. This pushes further back the recognition that the company needs jump-start marketing. If they push jump-start marketing further back, they experience more layoffs until, finally, the CEO is laid off.

When the going gets rough, even if it is caused by a bad economy, it is indeed time to use jump-start marketing. In most cases, this would also mean *increasing* the number of salespeople.

What would happen if the principles of jump-start marketing were used when the economy was good, if the company was already prospering? Wow! Think what Wall Street would do then!

A Simple Test You Can Take

(Fill in the blanks.) **A knee-jerk reaction when the going gets rough is to _____ employees. The better strategy is to _____ salespeople.**

(Fill in the blank.) **If a salesperson brings in $100 and the cost is $10, when would you stop adding salespeople?**

Answers

1: Layoff. Hire.

It's sort of like going on a month's vacation to some plush resort. The food is plentiful, terrific, and loaded with fat and calories. Almost anybody would say, I'll enjoy this a bit and then go on a diet when I get back. When times are good, companies can get bloated. Then they can go on a diet. A diet doesn't necessarily mean a starvation diet. For a business, a diet could mean not filling a position when it becomes vacant. In today's world, companies don't think of diets, they think of major surgery. This type of surgery doesn't just cut away the fat. It cuts into the bone.

When times are good, businesses have to protect themselves from binge hiring. Since I have usually been involved with businesses that show tremendous growth, I have had one rule of thumb about hiring non-salespeople when times are good.

The core condition of my rule of thumb is that I try to hire people who have a great work ethic. When I'm successful at that, I work at providing them with enough work and opportunity to challenge them. Only when they are approaching the point of working too hard over a period of time—where there will be diminishing returns—will I hire somebody to lighten the load. Thus, the work already has to be there. If eight people had been handling the work of ten people, I'll hire a ninth person. This will allow them to do the work of eleven people.

Using this philosophy, it's difficult to overhire non-salespeople.

2: A while ago, a secondary sports league asked me to speak to their top executives. A secondary sports league is any league that isn't the NFL, the NBA, Major League Baseball, or the NHL.

To illustrate my point about hiring ticket salespeople, I again used currency. Instead of using pesetas like I did in Spain, I used dollars. Before I went into this, I asked how many of the executives had risen to their position through a background in finance. About half of the executives raised their hands.

"Okay, this little demonstration is only available to those that raised their hands," I said. I then pulled a $10 bill out of my pocket and waved it to the group.

I asked, "Who will give me $1 for this $10 bill?"

Nobody responded. They just sat there.

There was no interpreter there to mess this up. I was asking in English to English-speaking people.

Finally, I singled out one guy and walked over to him. "Do you have a dollar?" I asked.

He did. He reached for it, but then held on to it.

"You can tell this is a financial guy," I said. "He's thinking about this. He's thinking about whether he should give up $1 to get $10. He's thinking of his dollar being an *expense* item. A marketing person would see this as a guaranteed investment. He gives me $1, I give him $10."

We made the exchange. I then asked him if he had another dollar. He did. I pulled out another $10 bill. "I'll trade you this $10 bill for your $1 bill."

This time, he was a little quicker with the trade.

"He's getting the hang of this," I said. "He's starting to think like a marketing person."

When trying to jump-start a company, you have to think as a *marketing* person. The finance person will have already cut into the bones of the company. Only marketing will give that company a life force.

19. IS IT FUN?

Ground rule #19: Jumping higher than you think you can is possible with jump-start marketing.

A long time ago, when you went to an NBA game and a team called a time-out, you'd see an old man with a broom sweeping the floor. Now it's dancers, mascots, lasers, and loud rock music.

Sometime between the old man with his broom and the dancers, the half-court shot for a free car was born. A fan would be chosen at random and ushered out to mid-court during a time-out. If the fan made the shot from half-court, the fan won a car. This was when a stripped-down new car cost about $3,000.

There were a lot of variations to that contest. Forget the cheap car: Back in 1981 while with the Portland Trail Blazers, we came up with the $100,000 shot. Safeway was the sponsor, and Al Neish loved it. The shot was attempted each game from three-quarters court. You make the shot, you get a hundred grand.

Nobody came close. All the shots fell way short. Most fans shot the $100,000 shot like they would a set shot. Nobody was that strong to make it. The only way to make the shot was to throw the basketball like a football. After the initial excitement of a fan shooting for $100,000, the futility of the shot led to boredom. It was like going back to the old man with the broom.

Back to the drawing board. We needed to make the target bigger. If we could get the fans to heave the ball to try to hit the backboard, it would at least have a chance of going in.

We restructured the contest. If the fan made the shot, the fan got the hundred grand. If the fan hit the backboard, the fan received two round-trip tickets on Alaska Airlines. The bigger target didn't help. Only one fan hit the backboard.

During the off-season, we had a think-tank session about this. You may wonder why we spent any time at all on a silly shot. Well, if we came up with the right promotion, it would be a fun diversion for the fans during a time-out.

During our think-tank session, the thinking went this way. We would build a ramp. At the end of the ramp would be a basket. Now, instead of shooting the ball seventy-five feet, the fan could *roll* the ball. The ball would roll down the court, up the ramp, and drop into the basket, which was four feet off the ground.

Anybody could do this. You didn't need to be a professional football quarterback to roll the ball seventy-five feet. There would be plenty of winners. Not for the $100,000, but Alaska Airlines offered two free round-trip tickets to anybody that rolled the ball into the hoop.

We built the ramp. We tried it out. Everybody in the office could roll the ball seventy-five feet and into the basket most of the time.

The ramp was on wheels, and during a time-out in our first game, we rolled it out. Our P.A. announcer told our fans about the contest. One lucky fan was escorted out on the court. To make sure we had a winner, we had preselected the fan and had him practice. He was flawless. Now, however, in front of a packed arena, he choked. He rolled the basketball, and it missed the ramp completely.

There was a smattering of boos.

The next game, we rolled the ramp out again. This time, we chose an attractive woman. She rolled the ball and missed by a mile. The fans lustily booed her.

We tried it the next game. Now the fans started to boo when they saw the ramp being wheeled out from underneath the stands. We picked out a radio station morning-drive disc jockey for the roll. He missed and was booed every step off the court.

Safeway was also the sponsor of the ramp. Al Neish didn't like to have his company booed. While our fans were having great fun booing, we knew the ramp had to go. Our Blazer fans were the best and most appreciative in the league. They would even politely applaud when the opposing lineup was announced. Now we were *teaching* them how to boo. What next? They might direct that new-found booing ability toward our players.

Yes, the ramp had to go. But let's have some fun on the way out. The next game we rolled out the ramp to standing boos. While the ramp was being rolled out, our ballboys scrambled out on the floor and put out three dynamite plungers. They then connected the wires from the dynamite plungers to the ramp.

Our P.A. announcer came out on the floor and said that we were going to blow up the ramp. A standing ovation! One "lucky" fan was chosen, and that fan had to choose which of the three plungers to use. Our fans were told that only one worked. If the ramp didn't blow up, then it would be back for the next game. The fans booed.

The fan started to walk toward plunger number one. Our fans were now starting to kibitz. No matter which plunger the fan picked first, it wouldn't detonate the ramp.

You see, we had contracted with a pyrotechnic wizard to rig up the ramp. The plungers were just for show. The actual blowing up would be started by our pyrotechnic wizard pushing a button on his remote control board. He was instructed only to blow up the ramp on the second plunger.

The fan picked a plunger and pushed. Nothing happened. Then, after a moment, the boos shook the building like thunder.

Our P.A. announcer shouted, "Should we give it another chance?"

The crowd cheered as loudly as they had booed. The players in the huddle on the bench straightened up and turned to see what all the noise was about.

The fan walked up to another plunger and pushed.

The pyro wizard pushed the button.

The ramp blew up. There was a loud teeth-rattling *kaboom* that came from under the ramp, and smoke billowed out. There were sparks and smaller *boom*s. A few oversized nuts and bolts rolled out from the ramp onto the floor. The crowd loved it. They cheered like we had just won the NBA championship!

We rolled the "blown-up" ramp off as the players walked back out to the floor. Our fans were still cheering. Our players got into it, and we rolled to a lopsided victory.

Our marketing manager had the ramp cut into small pieces. He said that if he didn't, I would have probably wanted to bring the ramp back for the April Fool's Day game.

I did keep a souvenir from the ramp. It is always in my office. It's not one of the nuts or bolts that rolled out. It's one of the mock TNT plungers. I keep it in my office to remind me that things don't always work out. Instead of belaboring that, it's better to just blow it up and go on.

■

Working in sports, we work during the week when other people work. We also work when other people play—at night and on the weekend.

There used to be seasons—I don't mean spring, summer, fall, winter, but baseball, football, basketball, and hockey. The seasons for each sport are now longer, the preparation for each season is more intense, the financial risks are much greater, and there is more pressure from fans, the media, agents and bankers, and in-house naysayers. Sometimes, the weight of it all starts to pile up on our shoulders.

Whenever I would get weary, I would think of just one thing. That one thing was a steel hat with a light on it.

A STEEL HAT WITH A LIGHT ON IT

Every day, people would put on that type of a hat, ride a cable car down into the Earth for a mile or so, and whack at some black rocks. Twelve hours later, they would get back on that cable car and ride back up. Twelve hours later, they would don that steel hat and do it all over again. When I get a mental picture of that, I'm delighted to be working when other people are working (nine to five during the week) and working when other people are playing (nights and weekends). Along the way, I think, Since I'm having the time of my life, I might as well have fun.

To have fun at work, I found two things were essential:

1: **A sense of humor.** This doesn't mean that we have to stand around the coffeepot cracking dirty jokes. It means taking a morbid situation like the New Jersey Nets and laughing about the Curse of Dr. J.

2: **Help make a company grow.** When a company is growing, everybody is more vibrant, more energetic. When a company is not growing, it's like donning that hat with a light on it and going into the ground for twelve hours. How much fun is that?

When a company isn't growing, there are really just two options: either use jump-start marketing or drag out the guillotine and start downsizing.

As we see in the news every day, downsizing seems to be the more popular method. Downsizing is quick. One simple memo can lop off a lot of employees. Downsizing is impressive to Wall Street for some morbid reason. These Wall Street analysts must think that downsizing is like playing the computer games Wolfenstein or Doom. But downsizing isn't Wolfenstein. Downsizing eliminates real people with real families and real bills.

Mostly, downsizing isn't really effective in jump-starting a company. Sure, in the short term, the bottom line does look better. But downsizing just delays growth. After all the blood is on the floor, eventually the company will have to at least *think* about growing.

Jump-start marketing is far more difficult than downsizing. One memo doesn't change the world. However, jump-start marketing is far more effective. It gets a company *growing*. It gets a company to be more *profitable*.

When a company is growing and profitable, it is far more fun. For the employees and for you.

HAVING FUN IN JERSEY

When I accepted the job as president of the New Jersey Nets, my friends looked at me as if I was stark-raving mad.

"That place is a *career killer*," one friend said. "You've had a terrific career and developed a great reputation with the Portland Trail Blazers, why in the world would you risk it on the Nets?"

Another said, "You're moving from the Great Northwest to

live in *Jersey*? If you were in the federal witness protection program, you'd be safe, because nobody, but nobody would ever figure somebody would make such a move."

The answer to those questions was pretty easy for me.

In Portland, the Blazers were a model franchise. The only knock that I would hear is that we were a "one-horse town" as in a "one-team town." Naysayers would say that, in that situation, anybody could be successful in marketing.

I knew, of course, that wasn't the case. We had created and developed marketing strategies in Portland that would be copied throughout the sports world. While I *knew* that those principles would work anyplace, I hadn't actually experienced it working in other places. New Jersey was the perfect place to see if jump-start marketing principles would work outside of Portland, Oregon.

Portland had one professional team. New Jersey—as part of the New York area—had nine pro teams. The Blazers were part of the fabric of the community. The New Jersey community had largely ignored the Nets. The Blazers didn't have a curse on them; the Nets had the Curse of Dr. J.

In taking the principles we developed in Portland to New Jersey, I discovered something strange. It was fun. I found that jump-starting a company through marketing was more fun than managing a stable company.

What made jump-start marketing fun for me should also make it fun for you. There are some pretty good reasons for that:

1: Jumping higher than you think you can. You can't jump high if you set the bar too low. With the New Jersey Nets, the bar was placed *way* up there. I could have just walked away and said that the bar was too high. Instead, we used jump-start marketing, which was like a little trampoline placed in front of the bar. After a couple of tries, we got up really high but barely nudged the bar off its peg. When we finally cleared it, we raised the bar higher and higher.

We cleared the bar again and again. That was fun! You'll find the same type of fun when you employ the principles and techniques of jump-start marketing. Sure, the bar now looks like it's stitched to the sky. But wait, let me put this little trampoline down. Now try it. You'll soar like never before, and you'll find out what fun it is.

2: Replacing scar tissue with beautiful blemish-free skin.
You may have seen those infomercials on TV where they're pitching skin cream that makes a person beautiful. Jump-start marketing works better.

When I started with the New Jersey Nets, the owners recommended that I "clean house." They said, "A lot of these people are lazy, not too smart, and just too comfortable." To listen to them, the front office staff was comprised of people who looked like the Wicked Witch of the West or the Hunchback of Notre Dame and were as bright as Rain Man.

I felt differently. I've never gone into a situation with blazing guns. I have always felt that people *wanted* to succeed, but that the systems in place didn't allow them to. We'd see what megadoses of jump-start marketing would do.

After a period of time applying jump-start marketing, people who were chronically late started to come in early. Other people who used to count down the last thirty minutes before 5:00 P.M. started to stay late. People started to come up with ideas on how we could improve.

The scar tissue that had accumulated over the years started to be replaced with beautiful skin. It wasn't an overnight transformation like the skin cream in the infomercial, it was a day-by-day, week-by-week process that made these people more vibrant, more interesting, far less cynical, and much more fun.

That's what happens when a company is in the jump-start marketing mode. The employees see, feel, touch, and dream success.

Seeing and experiencing all of this makes it fun.

3: Seeing young superstars grow without the fear of Kryptonite. We had hired a small army of people in their early to mid-twenties. We couldn't wait for them to naturally develop—we needed their energy, enthusiasm, and brains right away. We put them on an accelerated growth program. We encouraged these young people to *try* things. We pushed their learning capacities.

During this process, we removed all traces of Kryptonite—which could have rendered them motionless. Kryptonite, in this case, was managing with a heavy hand, jumping on their mistakes, limiting their initiative.

The results were astounding and fun for them and me and the rest of management. My feeling is that a minimum of five of these young people will become a VP-marketing of a major league team within ten years.

SILLY PUTTY

Remember Silly Putty? It was a lump of clay-like stuff that came in a plastic egg. You could press this stuff down on a newspaper, and it would somehow grab some of the ink off the paper to provide a mirror image on the clay. Silly Putty was supple, so you could mold it or shape it to any form. Silly Putty was fun.

Take the ideas of jump-start marketing and mold and shape them to fit your company or department. When you start to mold these ideas to your company or department, you'll find that your company will grow, your employees will grow, and *you* will grow. You'll find that this is fun.

So take off that steel hat with a light on it. C'mon, let's have some fun!

A Simple Test You Can Take

(Choose one.) **Which is more fun to do?**

A. Working in a coal mine whacking black rocks.

B. Working for a company that is not growing and facing downsizing.

C. Working for a company that is growing through jump-start marketing.

Answers

1: There is only one question on this last little test. If you think it's more fun to go into the Earth and whack black rocks, go do it. I applaud people who do those types of jobs—I was a spot-welder for awhile a long time ago. I know that those jobs bring a whole new definition to the word "work."

If you think it's more fun to downsize a company, then may the Curse of Dr. J be transferred to you.

If you chose (C), then I've got just two words for you. I would use these two words when I would end a meeting. It's a short phrase that I lifted out of an old John Wayne or Gene Autry movie.

Let's ride.

AFTERWORD
World-Class

I think it's great that when Charles Dickens wrote *A Tale of Two Cities*, he was actually thinking of the New Jersey Nets. Don't get caught up in the data that Dickens wrote *A Tale of Two Cities* over 100 years before the New Jersey Nets even existed. He was just ahead of his time. Albert Einstein surely could explain that.

So the last anecdote is Charles Dickens's tribute to the New Jersey Nets.

It was the best of times, it was the worst of times, it was the age of wisdom, it was the age of foolishness, it was the epoch of belief, it was the epoch of incredulity, it was the season of Light, it was the season of Darkness, it was the spring of hope, it was the winter of despair, we had everything before us, we had nothing before us, we were all going direct to Heaven, we were all going direct the other way . . .

■

When I first started as president of the New Jersey Nets, I told the owners that my goal was to help make the Nets a world-class franchise. A couple of the owners rolled their eyes.

At the first staff meeting, I said the same thing. A couple of employees laughed out loud.

Less than a year later, the owners and Nets employees could see, hear, and feel that the hapless Nets were indeed heading in the *direction* of world-class status.

One of the owners told me, "At the board of governors meeting [owners from each team], nobody would ask our advice on anything. Now different owners stop us and ask us things about how in the world we're turning this around."

While the owners have their meetings in the NBA, the employees have a different set. These meetings would cover areas that ranged from ticket marketing to public relations to sponsorship sales. Normally, teams would send about five to seven employees. The Nets employees used to slink in the meetings and sit in the back row. After we injected jump-start marketing, these same employees would walk in with a bit of a swagger and sit up front. No last row for them!

The team, of course, had not gotten any better. We were still lousy. Our roster was still filled with players that didn't enjoy playing basketball or competition. To give you an example of this, toward the end of the season one of our players came in to see Willis Reed, our general manager.

"I'd like to go home early," the player said.

"What do you mean 'go home early'?" Willis asked.

"My house is in San Antonio, and I'd like to go tomorrow to open it up and air it out."

"You can't do that," Willis said. "We've got eight more games left on the schedule."

"So, we'll lose them all."

Willis sternly told the player that he had to play those games, that he couldn't go home early.

The next day, the player reported that he had a bad back. Unlike a broken bone or a torn ligament, a "bad back" is a difficult injury to isolate and see. The standard procedure was to send the player to the team's doctor, which we did. The team doctor said that there was nothing obvious, such as a bulging disc. It was probably just a muscle strain. The player wanted a second opinion from a back specialist. That specialist happened to be located in San Antonio. The player missed the remaining eight games. The house in San Antonio got opened up and aired out.

Even with this type of player, I felt that our marketing successes could have gone on forever.

We knew our market.

We knew who we were.

We knew the team wasn't going to bail us out.

We were steeped in innovation.

Yes, we could continue with our marketing successes forever.

FAULT LINE IN JUMP-START MARKETING

The word "world-class" started to come around and haunt me. I knew that we would never reach world-class status with a lousy team. As much as I tried to see just a glimpse of hope in the future for the team, I couldn't see any. All I saw was the type of player that the Nets historically placed on their roster, and that gnawed at me. It bothered me that that gnawing was getting to me. After all, when I became the president of the Nets, I knew that my vote on player personnel decisions counted as much as your vote. You, of course, didn't have a vote.

When I signed on, I knew that the team was hapless without a decent past and a decent future. However, this was the perfect laboratory to prove the principles of jump-start marketing. We proved it. And proving it brought to the surface a fault line that meanders through jump-start marketing.

If you try some of the techniques in this book, you will find that jump-start marketing works. But as you achieve success in marketing products that are not the best, you will find that you automatically raise your sights. You could continue to successfully market these products, but now you will want to use those jump-start marketing principles to market a *better* product. Maybe even an *almost-the-best* product.

This fault line has given me a different perspective on jump-start marketing. Jump-start marketing can be two different things:

1: Success for almost forever. By injecting jump-start marketing, you can be more successful for a long time. It's not just a temporary quick-fix. It can be a continuing corporate lifestyle that guarantees success. Over the years, your product will get better, but it doesn't need to be the *best* to succeed year after year.

2: World-class foundation. Jump-start marketing buys you time to develop into a world-class company.

Let's look at it this way. Using jump-start marketing, you can boost a product that is not the best. You can boost it for a long time. While you're doing this, you can be developing a much better product. This product may turn out to be the *best* product in its field. Think of what this means. You've learned how to be successful with a product that is not the best. Using the same jump-start marketing principles, think what you could do with a *nearly-the-best* or *best* product? World-class!

RIDING ON

My contract with the Nets was for two years, ending in March 1995. After two years as a consultant to the Nets and two years as their president, I felt it was time to ride on. However, because there was the specter of labor unrest, I didn't feel comfortable in riding on into the sunset. I stayed on a month-to-month basis until there was an agreement between the NBA and the players' association.

On September 1, 1995, agreement was at hand, and I resigned. We were going back to Portland, Oregon.

The transition back to Portland was simple. We had never sold our house in Portland, nor "The Nugget House" on the beach. My wife and I just got on an airplane at Newark Airport and flew home.

Two weeks later, I was in Ireland, playing golf in the wind, drinking a few Guinnesses, and writing this book. As I wrote this book, I accepted some consulting jobs with several pro sports teams. Jump-start marketing worked as well in those areas as in New Jersey.

Eventually, you might see me lead a team again. If I do, move to that market. Buy season tickets. It might not be evident at first, but you will have bought tickets to a budding world-class team.

Think of the fun you and I will have.

Index

resignation from Portland, 183
rubber chicken/letter, 214-18
and secondary sports league, 250
and Spanish basketball league,
    240-42
and sports writers, 199-204
Spoelstra, Watson, 71-72, 121-23
Sponsorships, 21, 44-46, 59, 166,
    168, 172, 174, 254
Sporting News, 121
Sports Marketing Case Studies, 66
Sports Marketing Evaluation, 66
Star Wars (movie), 71
Stern, David, 99, 184
Sweepstakes, as marketing tactic, 152

Tale of Two Cities, A (Dickens), 263
Terrorist group for innovation, 94-95
    and hype, 105, 108

and naysayer, 106, 108
start-up steps, 100-105
unprepared presentations, 107
"Think tank" sessions, 76-78, 88, 95
TicketMaster, 33-34, 35
Time magazine, marketing sugges-
    tion, 149-51
Toronto Raptors, 98

United Airlines, 231
University of Houston, 139
Up-selling, 111, 113

Vancouver Grizzlies, 98

Walton, Bill, 167
Weinberg, Larry, 183
White Castle Family Night, 208-9
Winnipeg Jets, 154